Copyright © 2024 by R. E. Emerlye

All rights reserved globally.

No part of this publication may be reproduced, distributed, or transmitted in any form or by any means, including photocopying, recording, or other electronic or mechanical methods, without the prior written permission of the publisher, except as permitted by U.S. copyright law.

Cover and Illustrations by Cynthia Emerlye.

ISBN: 978-1-7345438-4-1

Published by Emerlye Arts LLC

Middlebury, Vermont

www.EmerlyeArts.com

Colored Into Carpe Diem

A Storybook Memoir

Emerlye Arts ®

The Peaceful Pages Collection

R. E. Emerlye

To Beauty,

My dear Mumsy.

Now, we shall never be apart.

TABLE OF CONTENTS

130618 MUMSY COLORING PAGE 7

PREFACE 11

I: THE FUTURE SHAMAN 12

II: YOUNG CYNTHIA 14

III: EDITH ADELAIDE 16

IV: SEVERINO SILVA 18

V: RECOLLECTION - THE PREMIERE 21

VI: MOUNT HOLYOKE 23

VII: BRUCE WARREN 24

VIII: RECOLLECTION – THE JOURNEY 28

IX: MOTHER CYNTHIA 31

X: DREAMS TO REALITY 33

XI: APPARITION 36

XII: DREAMWALKER 39

XIII: GIFTS FROM MOAB 42

XIV: RECOLLECTION – GIVEN TO PAUSE 45

XV: SPIRITUAL COLLAGE 47

XVI: RECOLLECTION – THE SEA CLIFF 49

XVII: RECOLLECTION – EGYPT 51

XVIII: EMERLYE ARTS BEGINS 53

XIX: RECOLLECTION - REUNITED 57

XX: RECOLLECTION – IMMORTAL BOND 61

XXI: RECOLLECTION – FOREVER 64

XXII: PRESENT TIME 66

XXIII: VERMONT CHILDHOOD 68

XXIV: COLORED INTO CARPE DIEM 70

XXV: GRASPING THE AWAKENING 72

XXVI: ADVENTURE 74

XXVII: SPIRITUAL FARMER 75

XXVIII: SANTA CRUZ 78

XXIX: RETURN HOME 80

XXX: LAND OF THE KNOWING	84
XXXI: TRANSCENDENCE	86
XXXII: ALLIGNMENT	89
XXXIII: EMERLYE	91
EPILOG	94

PREFACE

Just as my mother Cynthia Emerlye's artwork blends reality with the vivid vision of her extraordinary creative mind, so too is this story a tapestry of truth interwoven with the magic of a fairytale.

Within these pages of my storybook memoir, my own past life recollections echo between chapters grounded in real historical events, bringing together the creation of Emerlye Arts from both my mother's life and my own, into today.

Like Paulo Coelho's *The Alchemist*, this story traces a journey to one's personal legend—how the evolution of my mother's healing gifts as an art medium brought us both to realize our most brilliant of destinies.

Each green-eyed girl is born a facsimile of her mother, alike her mother before her. This time, it is I, the next on the journey. Emerging from a dream, I am here to seize the day.

I: THE FUTURE SHAMAN

When the nanny came to take the kids, Cynthia felt obliged to follow through. She had everyone dressed in Sunday clothes piling into the van—everyone except the youngest, who the new friend said she could bring along to where they lived far away in the Moab desert.

Cynthia and her daughter traveled in a separate car following behind their acquaintance, making the journey from Salt Lake City down to otherworldly small western homes, set aside a backdrop of jagged red rock formations.

When they finally arrived, the long, silent greeting Cynthia received at the door was difficult to withstand. The woman who brought them gave a delayed introduction:

"This is my mother; she is one of our tribal shamans."

Cynthia wondered if the lady who had organized the meeting had mentioned she would be bringing visitors. The three-year-old in her arms clung to her.

The hut where the Native American grandmother lived was modern compared to the ancient sand and clay landscape, yet still appearing weathered with age.

The home faced the desolate, unpaved road they had traveled. It was small, with a door in the front, flanked by coniferous trees and an oasis of cacti decorating the porch in different sized pots near the entrance.

An educated artist, Cynthia corrected her first thought: of course this shaman's abilities were unchanged by her gender, though hollywood often pictured medicine men. Then her mind wandered to her own clothes, the high-collared dress she had worn to church, feeling suddenly overdressed in the desert heat.

She suspected the little house had no air-conditioning like her posh new condo. She felt hot holding her daughter, who was also overdressed after Sunday school, and made a mental note to remove the girl's shoes and stockings as soon as possible.

At the door, the aged shaman stood transfixed. She wore a long gray skirt, falling just above her ankles, under a burgundy T-shirt with a lifelike wolf painted on the front. Barefoot except for leather sandals, she was adorned with large Navajo silver jewelry set with stones on her wrists, fingers, and neck. Her long black hair was braided once and tied with carved wooden beads that clinked softly when she moved.

Cynthia considered that perhaps the woman had in fact expected visitors, based on her well-kept appearance. She smiled and presented her toddler politely.

The old woman stared at the small girl, ignoring the greeting. Her eyes were deep and ageless, her mouth set in thin purple lips. Her long hair hung forward over her shoulder. She had a straight, elegant nose and a heart shaped jawline—a face where age continues to define its beauty.

No emotion could be seen as she did not return the smile.

The gatekeeper seemed to be allowing herself time to assess the situation. It felt as if the visitors might not be allowed in.

The old matron and the young child looked straight at each other for a long moment, leaving the two young women beside them uncomfortable.

The girl, who also had her mother's olive complexion and emerald eyes, peered right back at the stranger. Though separated from her siblings now, her tiny dress was hand-sewn by Cynthia with care to match her siblings on Sunday's such as this. Her auburn hair braided into short pigtails.

At last, the shaman broke her gaze.

Her own daughter urged her—surely, they could find something to talk about if she would just give it a chance. She reminded the group about her own little girl inside, suggesting the children could play together.

Seemingly unmoved, the grandmother held her post for one last quiet moment before stepping aside. Finally, everyone was permitted to cross her threshold.

The shaman shut the door behind them.

II: YOUNG CYNTHIA

Forsythia suspensa, a tough garden plant that blooms just as warm spring emerges from cold winter.

During her early life, Cynthia felt she was caught in a kind of suspense, waiting for moments when she was free enough to grow into her true desires. The weight of many responsibilities pressed on her young shoulders, yet within her she carried hidden treasures—moments of spiritual awareness that she guarded and cherished. She believed these secret flashes of knowing were the truest descriptions of her inner self. But as the eldest child, she also bore the responsibility of being ever-available, always dependable.

A devoted, patient spirit, Cynthia was capable of extraordinary goodness, giving of herself beyond self-interest. When her life's duties seemed to conflict with her soul's longings, she often chose to quietly set aside her aspirations, accepting what was required of her without complaint.

Her childhood home was a two-story farmhouse with a weathered barn on twenty acres in rural Vermont. Its address—Cloudland Road—suited the place perfectly then and still does today. From there, Cynthia learned the rhythm of a daily journey: walking a few miles along a path which carried her down to a winding dirt road, through hayfields that bent in the wind, over an iron bridge arched like a doorway into enchantment. Other children joined along the way, drifting in from their own woodland trails.

Most mornings the girl wore a pastel frock tied with a bow at the back, covered by an apron sewn by her grandmother, layered carefully over her favorite jumper.

Woodstock, the town she traveled toward, was a place preserved in time. Colonial homes stood with rustic post-and-beam frames, chimneys sending up woodsmoke into crisp skies, each brick-and-mortar hearth weathering centuries of Vermont winters. It was a setting steeped in endurance and charm.

On this day, as she strolled homeward, a single hummingbird and a small company of butterflies fluttered after her, drawn to her floral details as though she herself were part of the blooming countryside.

Cynthia's doll-like beauty carried a sweetness that only amplified her presence: her dark wavy hair pinned back with a sterling clip, olive skin tanned by long days in the garden. Recently, she had discovered the art of escape—slipping outdoors under the excuse of weeding rows of vegetables, only to stretch herself out in the sun and nap among the green.

Keeping a slow pace, she lifted her mother's green eyes toward the light, watching sunbeams flicker through swaying branches. Then suddenly, without clear cause, a strong breeze rushed in. Cynthia did not fight against it. She let it carry her. She let her dress fly, spinning herself round and round in surrender to its pull, twirling until dizzy and laughing, as if the wind itself were her dance partner.

Finally, breathless, she collapsed into a hayfield, curling into the tall grass like a young deer bedding down. Her wrinkled dress bunched beneath her, her small carpetbag of schoolbooks became a pillow, her long chocolate-brown hair spilled out in waves around her face. White moths circled delicately above her as she lay watching.

She thought of her twelfth birthday, just passed. She wondered what was different now about growing older. And as she gazed around, it seemed wildflowers were blooming everywhere—flowers she had never truly noticed before on her hurried walks. *Had they always been there?* A sudden truth dawned: there was more to life than she had seen. The details contained entire worlds, if she only stopped to look.

So, she remained still. A quiet decision formed inside her: to pause, to rest, to be simply with herself. The feeling was liberating, a freedom she had never tasted with such intensity before. Her emotions swirled with the fading rush of the wind, her spirit lifting as though set loose.

Watching the clouds drifting above, her breath slowed. Yet excitement lingered within—what was this beauty she felt flowing into her? Could it be something meant not only for her to enjoy but also to one day share with others?

The birds sang on. A warmth bloomed from within her, growing steadily. It was as if an ancient knowledge had been planted deep inside her and was now awakening. *Everything is connected,* she realized. The sun's rays on her skin and the light she felt glowing from her heart were the same force. She was rekindling something she had always carried: a bond with all the beauty that threads through the universe.

Cynthia did not yet know that she was a catalyst—that her life would serve as a channel for something divine, conspiring to unfold through her. She did not yet know that her soul's eternal name was *Sundara*, meaning beauty itself, nor that she would become an embodiment of love and gratitude, unable to keep from pouring those frequencies into the world.

But the truth was there, glimmering in the grass that afternoon. She had walked this earth before. She was weaving, once again, a thread she had begun in lifetimes past.

Years later, this child of Vermont hayfields would awaken portals that bound Earth to the Great Universe, offering art as the key. For now, she lay unaware, destined to forget her eternal past until her final days.

But she was Cynthia Ann, the first Emerlye, and even then, her dreamquest was guiding her forward—instinctively, steadily, dreamwalking reality into being.

III: EDITH ADELAIDE

A woman with dark brunette hair walked down the winding streets of Libya, her bright red lipstick accentuating her light eyes—a perfect shade to bring forward the rouge in her golden complexion.

She was tall, slender, with slight curves in all the right places, and wore an outfit specially tailored for her: a finely crafted three-piece dress suit in light gray, paired with a crisp white blouse. A violet scarf was elegantly tied around her long, graceful neck. In those days, one's social standing could still be discerned by attire. Hers reflected a life of comfort.

The woman's confident bearing hinted at intelligence. Focused on her destination, a small boy skipped at her side, holding her left hand, while she cradled another child on her right hip. They seemed in a hurry, yet composed and prepared for wherever they were headed—until, suddenly, another woman rushed to block their way and, without warning, slapped the young mother across the face.

Shocked, the mother froze. She rubbed her cheek with her left hand and set the other child down beside his brother. The stranger who had struck her barked something loudly, then in a raspy whisper.

The mother raised her gloved hands defensively, trying to break the tension, searching the woman's face for any recognition. Only her long, voluminous skirt shielded the two boys, who tucked themselves into its folds like a curtain.

The mom could not understand what the outburst was about—she did not know Libyan Arabic. The stranger kept repeating, "Pariji, Pariji!"

Little heads peeked up to watch the scene. At last, the upset woman calmed. With no way to decipher the meaning, the mother straightened, shook her head, and departed with her children in tow.

Her name was Edith Adelaide. Raised as the only girl in a small family, she was the obedient daughter of two world travelers, Angelina and Severino.

At eighteen, Edith had married a man who promised both comfort and adventure. Her yearning for such a life mirrored her immigrant father's ocean crossing to meet her mother—except this man had never crossed any distance for her. The more available she made herself, the less he seemed to remain still.

That day, Edith came to understand—painfully—that following her husband led her into places where she was never truly at home. In his shadow, she saw he was never searching for the belonging she craved.

The slap had been more than a physical blow; it was a metaphor for awakening. After years of traveling the world to broaden their small life, she had had enough.

Miss E.A. Silva—before marriage and young children—had been a modern woman in the forties and fifties, devoted to exploring the depths of her unique spiritual existence. But now, her spirit longed for something steady.

Constant travel had not expanded her sense of self—it had diminished it. Her kind partner understood her need to follow her soul's call, even as he recognized her growing depression. The stability she desired could not be easily provided by him.

In addition to their two sons, Edith and her husband, Paris, had two daughters at home. She knew their little ones needed long-term friendships more than anything, so she and Paris agreed to return her and the children to the United States, where they could regain a sense of belonging.

Ultimately, Edith planned to live in New England, near her parents in Rhode Island. Her soon-to-be-ex-husband purchased a family home for them and, generously, placed it in her maiden name.

With her kids gathered close, Edith summoned the fortitude to follow her own guidance again. She would chart her own path, letting dreamwork and intuition lead her. Though she never fully understood the gift, those practices are part of what she had already done to draw in a great and powerful immortal spirit, named by the world as Sundara to be born as Edith Adelaide's eldest daughter.

IV: SEVERINO SILVA

Edith's mother, Angelina, loved her charismatic husband, Severino. He had come from Cape Verde, an island off the coast of Africa. His father, a land baron there, led and cared for his tenants like a patriarch loves his own family. Silva recalled details like this to his sweetheart later in life, once he found her. The man expressed that his father was a good man, one who trusted his intuition while making difficult decisions regarding many people's lives.

Silva retold his story many times, describing how, before leaving the island, his father had watched him grow into a man ready for maturity. Though it seemed time for responsibility when others looked on, many moments in Severino's youth showed his longing for adventure rather than the duties his elders expected.

Unable to follow his father's sterling example, fear struck. Severino felt a fool for allowing lust to distract him from retaining freedoms in life. At the time, he could not see that his intense physical desires were not impeding his path to a greater destiny. He recognized only slightly the responsibilities his father had been coaxing him toward with the arrival of a new baby—his contrasting spirit pining to explore the world.

With the wisdom of hindsight, Severino recalled himself as a maturing boy, at a troubling juncture in life, choosing to follow his spirit over society's rules. It was an act of defiance when he pursued the physical, yet that choice guided him toward lessons no societal law could teach.

His young future held consequences. Surrounded with love, the youthful mother of Severino's infant found herself supported by her own mother and grandmother, leaving little need for his presence. The impact left the teenage boy in shock, unsure how to navigate life outside tradition.

Severino's fears forced the new grandfather to decide Severino's path.

Most assumed he could never return when the boy was sent to the Americas. Now, he knew his parents made a hard decision together. Though they loved their son dearly, their boy and the girl he had chosen were abandoning a long-established way of life.

The elders had taught all the children that community law, interwoven with the spiritual universe, brought balance. Yet individual needs would always arise when survival demanded. Such wisdom guided their faithfulness to the people.

The young couple wished to remain on Cape Verde but, following childbearing, desired separate lives, abandoning tradition. Silva senior decided that the right example was to allow his eldest heir to advance with a life shaped by his spirit.

***

When the day came for Severino to depart, he embraced his mother. She gave him a small leather portfolio filled with pages to record and share his endeavors. Tucked within were loose sheets for letters to be sent home.

His father sent him with a satchel of coins, dried fruits, wild boar jerky, goat cheese, and other island morsels.

"A leader must admit his faults to become great," he said. "I admire you for acknowledging your capabilities."

Walking him to the ship, his father continued, "We follow ancestral laws. To be guided by your spirit is in your blood. My commitment is to this island and its people; yours is to discover your path." The boy shuddered and wept, yet understood.

After their embrace, his father added, "Change brings fear. You will have safe passage, my ocean son. Keep conscious in the experience of life. Follow your soul's instinct, and you will remain close to your heritage."

His mother ran back, repeating, "Remember you are loved, Severino."

The ship's captain rested a hand on the boy's shoulder as he boarded. From afar, his father called, "Follow the future your heart seeks. Your best outcome will not be found in the past. You are my son… Go now, and do not return."

Pushed from his birthplace by the birth of his first child, Severino sailed toward his fate across the vast ocean, hoping his spirit would strengthen.

A month later, amidst a storm, Severino recalled his father's instructions. Sitting in pause during the harsh weather, he reviewed the journal. Without knowing it, he practiced a spiritual guidance of self-transition, leading himself on a dreamwalk across great waters toward maturity.

Though familiar with boats, this journey was to be an epic one. Traveling to Boston, a land of opportunity, he learned balance: freedom with home life, flexibility within responsibility. Rather than harboring a grudge toward his parents, Severino accepted his fate and grew in purpose. Occasionally, he missed the stability of island life, yet he embraced the adventure ahead with gratitude.

Throughout his travels, Severino recorded his awakening experiences. By the time he reached New England, his journal reflected love for what was and what would become. Sketches of native flora and folklore adorned his pages. The gift from his mother had allowed him to manifest guidance through inner reflection, fostering spiritual growth.

***

When Severino met his love, Angelina Gonsalves, at Boston harbor, he recognized his spirit of adventure reflected in her. They married, embracing a home life that balanced freedom with stability. Together, they continued their journaling, folding new pages into Severino's treasured leather portfolio.

Letters were sent to both their island families, sharing news of marriage, home, and family. Silva's fondness for cooking revealed a return to the way of his father, blending care, tradition, and creativity.

Transplanted to Rhode Island, Severino commuted to work on ships that tugged vessels in and out of the harbor, sometimes bringing home massive fresh fish or preparing meats he would cure in soil at home for later meals upon his return. These acts reflected both practicality and a cultural expression of giving. The Silva household became the heart of its block, hosting gatherings where generosity and joy flourished.

The couple soon welcomed three children, including Edith Adelaide. Together, Severino and Angelina understood a vital truth: sometimes, a journey must abandon the known to follow an unpredictable path.

One special night, watching Edith's free spirit, they recognized greatness being nurtured simply by allowing authenticity to bloom. Sitting around the dinner table, with laughter and tears of unexplainable joy, the Silva family celebrated life fully, a legacy of adventure, love, and spiritual intuition passed through generations.

V: RECOLLECTION - THE PREMIERE

In my first memory of another life, the day is warm but not hot. The sun is out. A soft breeze moves through the surrounding flowering trees and bushes. Close by, two sweet children with jet-black eyes and dark, curly hair wave, just as the wind stirs the grass.

Lying on soft floral beds, the children sense they are between the earth and the stars. Fluffy clouds, like castles above them, blanket their existence in this vast field.

I watch them, and yet I know them. I know the way their laughter rises in perfect harmony with the rustling leaves, as if the trees themselves are keeping rhythm. I feel the old ache of recognition, that unshakable familiarity that tells me I am not witnessing strangers.

I see these two young scions stand again, walking hand in hand, giggling, then running further into an open space where a grand tree stands alone. Their wild manes whip freely in all directions, the wind a friend pulling them toward adventure.

Suddenly, they look back and smile at me—then at each other. It becomes clear that I was once one of them.

Now, I see myself: sitting in the field, breathing hard, laughing, looking at my dear beloved one. We've fallen back onto our elbows, resting in the shade of the old-growth tree at the border of a place we know is an entryway into the ether; the place where this memory, and all others, began.

The vision feels near; time has not dimmed it. I understand that my dreams and the introduction to this special other began here, in this precious premiere.

In my mind, the nearby cliff appears—the one we've run to before—but this time, we remain grounded beneath the tree. I know without looking that the view overlooks the tireless motion of the sea.

The morning has dawned. We release our hands. I lie back, letting the earth hold me, my fingers sinking into the sandy loam beneath the grass. My partner's spirit looks at me as her hands draw designs in the soil between us.

She and I are awake in the earth's love for life. A thread seems to run from her heart to mine, woven of the same love we feel for all beauty in the universe. I mirror her attention outward, toward the world.

Beauty itself brings with it the power of love from the Great All, she whispers.

I am mesmerized by the muted clouds overhead. Without realizing how, I am transported to a place within me beyond speculation—where only observation remains.

The memory shifts; I now hover above my ancient self, drifting over the grand tree and the open meadow untouched by human hands. The tree, eternal, drops seeds that grow deep in its own root system, immortal if left undisturbed.

The recognition is clear: part of what I see exists on the distant side of all life. Releasing the desire to know more, I feel instead—just as intricate dreams make sense before waking into daily confusion.

I notice my diaphanous clothing floating around me, dissipating into mist as I drift in the wind. I am in every perspective, beyond time, feeling the precious levels of existence.

Quenched with soul-deep nourishment, I return to myself. Awakened on my bed of flowers, I watch her continue drawing—bringing her art from the ether into the physical. This is my first memory of understanding why her soul's name is Sundara.

The sound of the ocean pulls me further into the moment. The water builds and breaks, endlessly repeating—reminding me that all endings become beginnings, and all is one.

For a moment, life finally makes sense to my heart and mind. Then thought creeps in, separating me from where I was. I close my eyes, centering in meditation to return.

Without speaking, I feel Sundara lying beside me, both of us in the land of knowing—past and present held together in the pattern of adventure leading toward the refinement of true beauty. And I know now what I did not then: this was not just a memory. It was the start of a map. A seed of a promise that would unfurl across lifetimes, until it brought me here, to this life, to her again.

VI: MOUNT HOLYOKE

"Off to college with you, girl!" Edith Adelaide told her eldest daughter, who was to become the first female in her family to earn a Bachelor's degree.

Cynthia Ann had a good head on her shoulders, and chose on her own to put herself into an all-girls' college. Mount Holyoke, in the beautiful hills of western Massachusetts, had once been a finishing school for young women to become proficient wives and mothers.

The times were the seventies, when women's rights were a loud, serious conversation everywhere. Liberal-minded Cynthia would later remark that equal rights for women became a "fun" subject only after the long struggle for liberation had been won. Always keeping history in mind, she reminded women who took their freedoms for granted that they stood on the winning side of a fight.

She wasn't wealthy enough for every luxury her new school offered, but she was thrifty and humble. After her first year in the dorms, she moved to a small attic apartment above a family home, three stories up. Most nights she lived on rice, beans, and potatoes—except when the kind family would invite her down for supper.

Neat, clean, and a straight-A student, Cynthia avoided anything illegal or reckless. At Mount Holyoke, she poured her creativity into writing plays, organizing events, and designing group activities with the festive flair she had inherited from her elders. She even petitioned the school to allow a new degree program—and succeeded.

The young woman specialized in language studies and production and began earning a small wage creating curriculum and organizing activities for local elementary schools. These early steps—blending education, art, and empathy—were the first signs of the art therapist she was becoming.

She hosted the college talk show now and then, and her artistic work began to be noticed in small gallery showings, hinting at the path her future would take. Her creative outlets mattered as much as her grades, so when she agreed to write a radio play for one of her classes, she approached it with seriousness.

One of her chosen actors, a male student admitted for a semester of co-ed integration, wasn't taking his role seriously. She put on her coat and scarf, marching across campus to the men's dorms to confront him. On the way, she cooled from anger to mild resentment, deciding instead to be grateful for the richness his deep voice would bring to her production.

The campus glowed with autumn leaves as she arrived at the vandalized dormitory door. Feeling annoyed again, she flung it open and called, "Bruce!"

—then stopped, closed the door softly, and tried again, "Hello? Does anyone know Bruce?"

A smirking young man peered from the stairwell. "Who?"

Cynthia realized the actor must have some other name he went by. She considered turning back, but pressed on into the noisy, messy dormitory, dodging offers of "help" from curious boys.

Finally, another student descended the stairs. "You mean Ralf," he said. "That's his nickname. Come on, I'll show you his room."

VII: BRUCE WARREN

Cynthia knocked on the closed door and found herself face to face with a tall, blonde, blue-eyed young man with a mustache, a mischievous glint, and a room that looked like a small disaster. Torn clothing lay in heaps, and behind him hung a swastika flag—quickly explained as a wartime relic his uncle had captured from Nazi Germany.

She got to the point. "You've missed most of the semester. Will you ever be at class?"

"Attendance isn't required," he said with a shrug.

She insisted he either show up or record his part for her play.

As he fumbled with his mismatched shirt buttons, they shared a quick laugh, then she left, cheekily calling back to him, "Hope to see you there, Ralf" on her way out.

***

When Bruce joined the radio show cast later, he played his small role well enough. The production went to air, earned a mention in the school paper, and the two crossed paths more often.

He began walking with her across campus, sharing his "greatest accomplishment": getting dressed for class at the last possible moment.

She was skeptical, but intrigued. She saw in him qualities she valued—playfulness, uniqueness, goodness—even if his penny loafers were mostly a way to avoid tying laces.

She asked about the flag again. He admitted it was partly for shock value, partly a family keepsake.

Cynthia was aware of his reputation as the "party king," but was drawn to Bruce's intelligence and charisma. While she lived quietly and worked toward her degree, he slowly wove himself into her daily life.

But Bruce's legend extended beyond his charisma and intellect—he and his best friend Tommy had a history at Moses Brown School, a reputation that lived on in whispered stories of wild parties and near-expulsions.

It all began during their final year, when Bruce and Tommy decided to throw the largest bash the all-boys school had ever seen.

Despite being known for their wild antics, they had managed to stay one step ahead of trouble, thanks to Bruce's quick thinking. When word of their final party spread like wildfire across campus, the headmaster, as usual, had threatened expulsion.

Tommy, with his usual carefree attitude, was ready to face the consequences. But Bruce had a different idea. Realizing they might finally be caught, he came up with a brilliant plan: he and his cohort had previously applied to colleges where they were accepted. For Bruce, his choice was Bowdoin College in Maine. He felt he knew that if they were admitted before the party, their escape from the looming expulsion would be guaranteed.

Bruce's plan worked, and as the final bash began to unfold in their dormitory, the students marched out of Moses Brown in a procession. They made their stand with the chant, "Don't hate, let them graduate!" This was the largest protest in the history of the all-boys boarding school, and it was led by the very same Bruce Warren and Tommy, the two students who had managed to escape expulsion by sheer cleverness and a little luck.

The protest was filled with excitement, rebellion, and defiance, but it was also the culmination of a friendship built on shared experience and an unspoken understanding of two boys pushing boundaries.

Subduing his past with Tommy now at Mount Holyoke, by the time they graduated, Bruce had embraced Cynthia's Mormon faith and they were engaged —a pairing of opposites, each secretly enchanted by the other's world.

***

Upon graduation, Edith offered her daughter money for a class ring. Cynthia— ever the artist—chose instead a delicate, rose-and-white-gold ring set with diamonds around a bright amethyst, a little flower of gemstones that would serve as her engagement ring.

The bride-to-be wanted also to make her own wedding dress. However, a short amount of days before the ceremony Cynthia was nearly in tears over the fine silk. She had spent countless hours sewing, and though it was a beautiful design, something felt off. The dress wasn't coming together as she had envisioned.

She was tired and frustrated, the weight of her impending marriage and all the decisions she had to make pressing down on her. In the midst of this emotional turmoil, she found herself crying, overwhelmed by the magnitude of the day ahead and the life that awaited her. She was alone in her small apartment, the dress lying unfinished before her, her heart heavy with doubt.

At that moment, her mother, Edith Adelaide, had planned to make her way over to visit. Edith had always been a strong, independent figure, and now she thought she'd come to offer her daughter the wisdom only a mother could provide. But hearing over the phone that her daughter was in such distress, she knew something more was needed.

Edi-Ann, Cynthia's younger sister, had been born with the same name as their mother—Edith. But what made Edith Adelaide's naming choice truly special was that she had bravely given her second daughter the same name as her own, choosing to call her "Edith" as a junior—a decision typically reserved for men in those days.

It was a bold, unconventional act of love and pride, a tribute to the legacy of her own identity. For Edith Adelaide, naming her daughter Edith was an assertion of strength, an acknowledgement of her own place in the world, and a way to pass down the name to the next generation.

However, to avoid confusion in a household with two Ediths, Cynthia's younger sister had been affectionately called "Edi-Ann" by most people. This playful nickname stemmed from her middle name, Ann, and it stuck as a way to distinguish between the two.

As Edi-Ann arrived, sent with love by their mother to check on her sister, the moment was infused with the kind of support and love only a sister could offer. But as Cynthia cried over the dress, unsure of how she would pull everything together, Edi-Ann's comforting presence was just the start of what would become a miraculous turn of events.

Then, as if guided by divine timing, the seamstress from down the road appeared at their door. This was a woman Cynthia had met briefly, but never expected to play such an important role in her wedding preparations. Yet here she was, almost as though the universe had sent her at exactly the right moment.

The seamstress knocked softly, and when Cynthia opened the door, the woman smiled warmly, as though she had known exactly what was needed.

"I heard you were working on your dress," the seamstress said, her voice calm and reassuring. "I thought you might need a little help."

With no hesitation, Cynthia welcomed her in. The two women quickly began to work together, and the seamstress—who was kind, patient, and skilled—took the lead, making gentle adjustments to the dress, easing Cynthia's worries with her steady hands.

Edi-Ann stood by, watching as the two women worked in perfect harmony. It was as though some greater power had orchestrated this moment—Cynthia's sister there for emotional support, and the seamstress there to provide the practical guidance that Cynthia so desperately needed.

As the two women worked, Cynthia began to relax. The pressure she had felt earlier began to lift. It was a turning point—an example of how, sometimes, the right help arrives at exactly the right time. What had seemed like an insurmountable task—finishing her wedding dress—was now a joyful experience, all thanks to the divine timing of the shop owner's unexpected arrival.

Together, they finished the dress with delicate precision, and Cynthia couldn't help but feel that it was more than just the helpful woman's skill—it was as if fate itself had intervened.

Edi-Ann stayed by her side throughout the process, offering words of encouragement and support. It was a moment of deep sisterhood, the kind of bond that transcends time and place, and a reminder that family—and unexpected blessings—can come together in the most miraculous ways.

***

On her wedding day, guests gathered under a flowered arch. Bruce arrived late, disappeared to search his car for a bowtie, and was nearly married barefoot until his father shoved his own shoes onto him. The quirky and playful nature of Bruce was on full display once again.

Cynthia saw Bruce at the altar, his big clown shoes barely fitting him. As he stood there with a half-smile, his bride couldn't help but laugh at how utterly ridiculous yet endearing he looked. She thought of his father, sitting barefoot in the crowd. The oversized shoes seemed to symbolize the carefree, misfit attitude that she had come to love about him.

She couldn't help but think about how silly it was to see him standing there—his shoes so large they barely stayed on his feet—but that was Bruce: always full of surprises and quirks that made him who he was.

As she walked down the aisle to music she had composed herself, she noticed small omens—a dove landing, a sunflower falling into her path—reminders of partnership, and joy.

Cynthia looked at Bruce, took his hand, and felt the weight of the amethyst ring from her mother.

VIII: RECOLLECTION – THE JOURNEY

More knowing surges forward. Guided by my desire for spiritual growth, I gather from previous moments, incarnations, dreams, and inklings of life. I am translating symbolisms from the present as well, using the combination to construct my existence.

All that has gathered in me begins to reveal a pattern. Another bit of the story comes to light — another past that might be important to remember. It brings reason so all the pieces can fall into place. Beginning to understand my overall purpose, I sense the cosmos align to guide me to help others see it too.

In what I've recalled, my bare feet leave prints as I step softly along a dirt trail made of the softest topsoil. The narrow way is alive with healthy greenery growing along its edges. Both rough and smooth stones of all shapes and sizes affect my balance. The passage requires part of me as I cross.

As a young traveler, I mosey along slowly, heel to toe, my spirit in tune with my body, awake with rushes of realization.

Although I breathe as an adolescent, I am also old — my soul having existed for several millennia. Yet someone lingers within my heart who has existed longer. She is coming from another level of understanding and bearing the ability to predict our reunions.

I know it is Sundara; I have known for a long time, but she is not with me in this memory. Although I don't understand our connection as clearly as she can, I feel I will see her again. I am content with that knowing — a twin without my other — growing through this memory of a lifetime because I am on my own.

A small and dainty human being, I absorb the love for the earth through the soles upon which I stand. Welcoming the moments of shade along the wild path, I know they are part of the recipe for the dawning of light. Each warmth is matched by a heat from within.

My human senses illuminate with recognition of all things reaching me by differing ways of connection. I happily imagine the Great All is nodding to reward me for recognizing my existence among its universe.

My excitement shows for every bud, thorn, bramble, branch, or stem. Every leaf that brushes me — touching my skin or catching my flowing dress — adds to my passage.

I recall my adolescence becoming hushed by mature sense. The important transition becomes just another layer in the puzzle of my existence. Noticing the smell of blooming flowers, the rush of a waterfall, the pine forest — I realize that without my body, I could not dreamwalk in this way, combining existence.

Interaction like this affects the turns of my reality, life's journey bowing kindly in extraordinary ways. I curtsy back in my steps forward through its wonders. The new relationships I am having with all things in these moments become my catalyst for understanding when it is time for conscious life, or time to let go and let be.

As I grow into the awakening, it is impossible to tell at precisely what point in my existence I became present — nor how many times I was born before this memory of a lifetime. Like a true center, its exactness cannot be located until the whole pattern reveals itself.

I now understand that my spiritual path, though expansive, is built on past lives and present choices, threading my identity into an intricate web that links me to all I've been and will be.

I know moving forward is my evolution. Whether I travel bravely or with hesitation, I notice that life is full of motion which opens to new opportunities.

Named by others in my previous life, I was Aadyha now and forever in my soul. I use the power of its adventurous meaning to carry myself valiantly forward, realized as one of life's many small goddesses by the awarded blessing.

The trail upon which I embark makes a labyrinth — a metaphor for my mind, body, and soul. The whole design unfolds into one grand masterpiece, just as it does for everyone. Recognition of this serendipity deepens the engravings of images in my recollections.

This labyrinth represents not only the winding path of my personal growth but the paths of all souls, intricately linked by the universal design.

There is a sense that I cannot skip over or ignore emotions just to hurriedly reach the goals of this embarkment. Instead, I must live through all that comes, thus bringing the relief that gives birth to genuine renewal.

The reveal arrives in waves of knowing after not knowing; then, I awaken, feeling the wisdom of experience threading itself into my soul's growth.

Coming from before written history, this endless avenue to intermingle with Sundara has been laid bare by all. Everyone waxes inward and wanes outward to or from one another, existing in the same levels of scope.

We are age-old, following a deeply ingrained trail of spiritual existence on Earth. This can be seen through our experience together. I have come to understand that our shared experiences—our collective wisdom—are a map we all follow, whether we consciously recognize it or not. We are all journeying together, each playing our part in the grand, unfolding story of life.

Every time I awaken to realize the correlation of memories, I know the path presents an even grander labyrinth of labyrinths for all of the universe.

I have acquired the understanding that the trail exists beyond its travelers, one unable to be without the other. Only by commencing upon it can anyone perceive its complexities, finding it has been drawn from many beauties on Earth — such as Sundara — beauties that reveal how we can color in, or get colored into, life itself. The colors, though distinct, blend into a masterpiece of interconnectedness.

Now it is unveiled that the recollections appear whenever I can truly absorb their gifts. This one shows me that only in my naked existence with the earth will I come closer to finding the utmost direction where I must go.

Walking, surrounded by the ultimate peaceful symphony playing around me, is a recurrence. Like déjà vu, I recognize the vision is repeated so it guides me each time to awaken. The earth, with all its beauty and challenges, continues to serve as my guide and teacher.

A knowing inside me shows I exist within choice. It is my acceptance to embody my spirit as Aadyha, apart from Sundara — who lets all flow without resistance to choose. Whenever intertwined, she is the innocent source of an epic revolution, whereas, humbly, I must be the warrior who brings aid to her triumph.

The balance between our roles—one as a teacher and one as the guide—is what will lead me forward into the world, helping others awaken to their own spiritual power.

With her absence, I see more clearly how our union carries home for all to uplift. Utilizing our breakthrough, they can be transported through the divine chasm our bond meaningfully opens from ether to reality.

IX: MOTHER CYNTHIA

Dreaming is a spiritual muscle. To strengthen it, every time you awaken, remain in the state of non-thinking, suspending disbelief for as long as possible, recording every detail of nonsense if you wish to learn the passageway to understanding.

Newly married, Cynthia believes she is wide awake while she sleeps in her bed. There's a feeling that the rules guiding the waking world are somehow absent in her dream.

She was following a path, much like walking out from the thicket down the enchanted isle to her marriage ceremony to Bruce.

She wore her wedding dress, this time adorned along the bottom with endless layers of bright floral embroidery, thicker and more colorful as it reached the edges. Atop her head was a very nice sunhat with flowers pinned on its side; lacy ribbons around the base dangled, twisting into her wavy hair.

Turning slightly, she was amazed by what she saw behind her. Cynthia had six dream children — four boys and two girls — dressed in clothes she somehow knew she had sewn for each. They matched the colors in her own ensemble. Or had she colored her dress after sewing theirs?

She felt these children following her along the path but, no matter how she tried, she could not turn to see their faces, nor could she remember where they were all headed.

All six were moving forward. At the front, she was having the greatest time leading them into the luscious world, each progressing at her pace. They seemed happy and interactive in her company.

The dreamer loved to find ways to show them things they might like along the way. Ahead, the maternal guide gestured to uplifting sights on her left and right, hoping to teach them to lift their gaze from the trail and notice beyond what was directly in front of them.

A doubletree, sharing one massive trunk deep in the ground, revealed the insight that her children would remain connected by their roots but grow to different heights. The grand view of mountains and valleys peeking out from behind the thicket showed how to look beyond crowded forefronts and see the wide-open world.

Cynthia's dream was full of examples like these. As if she were a schoolteacher leading her young flock of students, she felt happily worn out trying to channel her gifts of knowing into their little souls. Even in sleep, she was rehearsing the role she would one day step into fully — the patient teacher, the inspired guide, the artist who would use color, form, and story to awaken others.

All of the children appeared very in tune with one another, despite walking separately. Now and then, a branch or stick would impede one of them or poke another, ensuring each had a unique experience of the path.

Inevitably, she predicted she would be the first to enter the middle of their journey. She planned to use that place — a sort of mezzanine — to pause and see each child more clearly, cherishing them individually before releasing them to walk their own paces beyond it.

The spiritual dream drifted into Cynthia awakening.

She turned to her antique bedside table, picked up a journal, and began to write every detail she remembered. Then she flipped back through earlier entries, piecing together fragments from several similar dreams.

The notes read: 'The weather is unnoticeable; that means nothing in our environment alters my ability to have all of my children, four boys, two girls.'

'Rachael will be dark and Heather will be light.'

'The boys all have gentle hearts.'

'I will name my first son after his father.'

Sweet Cynthia laid her head back into her feather pillow, feeling she was in heaven — peaceful now that she had happily decided her life was going to unfold great beauty from both around and inside of her.

X: DREAMS TO REALITY

Cynthia's new husband loved that her dreams had already revealed their plan to have six children. The newlyweds moved frequently after college; however, that didn't stop them from beginning their family.

This was during the late 1970s and early 1980s. They started off in the North so Bruce could take more business classes at the University of Chicago. The new father and entrepreneur opened a computer restoration business—a concept far ahead of its time.

Every day, Cynthia returned home from errands to walk up three flights of stairs to their two-bedroom apartment. By now, her blonde, blue-eyed infant, Bruce Warren Junior, was secured in a baby backpack for her to carry along with the groceries, and she was already expecting again.

No matter where the young family moved, despite whatever challenges arose, they kept two steady goals intact. First, they would dress as a formal business couple while searching for work for Bruce, and second, they would attend a local LDS Temple for Sunday service.

Cynthia's visions continued to recur while she practiced her mother Edith's techniques of transcribing them on paper at home to aid her method of dreamwalking—tying all spiritual symbols and insight together based upon seeking answers to her own questioning. The young mother never revealed her method at church for fear of judgment.

In the coming years, she chose her children's first and middle names based on her dreamwalks and by feeling each child's unique energy as they came into her life. She was keen to meet every dear newborn soul as though they had come especially to be with her.

While still living in Chicago, their second child was born. Cynthia saw such a sweet smile on her new baby girl's face, yet after labor, she was deeply conflicted about the girl's name.

All babies appear a sort of red color at first. Was this child Rachael or Heather?

The doctors requested the newborn's name for two days until one morning, Cynthia awoke with the certainty of who had come into her life. For just a second, she saw Warren's blue eyes in his sister's gaze, confirming this child would have a light complexion like her brother. There was no more doubt—Cynthia would continue to wait for the children who resembled her. She named the precious girl Heather Rosamond, giving the patriarchal grandmother's title as her middle name.

This baby was colicky, constantly crying and squirming. She could only be held facing outward, her stomach to the world. In nature, Heather is a type of wildflower. Growing into her brave toddler years, she got into all sorts of mischief, challenging her young parents to keep her safe.

On the most trying of mornings, Cynthia would find Heather in front of open cabinets, drinking liquids she had found under the kitchen sink. Her little red-haired, blue-eyed daughter would burp bubbles uncontrollably, signaling a visit to the local poison control office.

***

The next chapter of the couple's life brought a move to Virginia, where Bruce and Cynthia welcomed their third child, Joshua William. He was a sweet, calm baby who rarely cried. Cynthia felt relief after the chaos with her first two children.

It seemed the family might finally settle into something more "normal"—until one early Sunday school morning.

Warren, as they always called their first child by his middle name, came running to his unsuspecting parents to read a story from a children's book. Shockingly, he was only four and had never been taught the alphabet.

Cynthia asked where he had learned to read. He replied simply, "Sesame Street." The child had taught himself by quietly watching the learning show each morning.

***

Before Cynthia and Bruce could settle into life with newborn Joshua, daughter Heather and their gifted eldest, they were expecting again. This fourth child's middle name would finally be given from Cynthia's side of the family.

Their growing household prompted Cynthia to send out her sweet, artistic newsletters once again. Because of Bruce's early interest in technology, Cynthia typed the family news on one of the world's first Macintosh desktop computers, bringing the letters to life in a modern, innovative way.

They welcomed Benjamin Paris.

After the first three children inherited their father's complexion and red or blonde hair, Cynthia was grateful to write to friends and family about this new baby. Born with his umbilical cord wrapped around his tiny foot, Benjamin already showed a full head of dark hair. Cynthia noted, "His poor foot is fully recovered, and it seems his eyes will resemble his grandmother Edith's."

The family was quickly expanding. With Joshua and Benjamin as Irish twins—born only fourteen months apart—they became inseparable brothers, tumbling and running together, forming the center of the household until the next child arrived three years later.

***

One early morning, as the sun rose, Cynthia experienced a lucid moment similar to her recurring dreams. Though raising young children had exhausted her, she sensed something special was happening.

It was Sunday. She felt as if she had already completed her morning routine, returning from a short catnap, with the previous hours slipping from her mind. She shifted onto her side, fluffing her feather pillows to gaze toward the rising sun. Slowly, her sight blurred into whiteout as she sank deeper, breathing softly.

Quietly, Cynthia refocused her eyes. Below the bright light, she saw herself in natural linen clothing, sitting alone in a rocking chair. Surprised, she looked down to find an olive-skinned baby swaddled in her arms. Shocked, she knew it was not Benjamin.

The infant wore a beautifully embroidered white christening gown with delicate lace edges and a soft angora rabbit hair blanket. A velvet bonnet with a tiny purple flower rested on her head, and silk ribbons fastened under her chin. Tiny hands wore little mittens, and every piece of clothing appeared hand-stitched with silken threads.

The bliss in the dream was intoxicating. Time seemed to stand still as Cynthia stared at her creation. Then, unexpectedly, she heard the child's name spoken by her inner spirit.

In that instant, she saw herself as the newborn, peering up at her own mother. She heard Edith Adelaide saying Cynthia Ann, which covered what she wanted to know. Curious, she looked into her daughter's green eyes, reflecting her own through generations.

Abruptly, Cynthia awoke, realizing the fantasy was not real, yet it lingered as a vivid memory.

***

The fifth child, Adam Stockwell, became the family's first New England baby. His complexion was light with red hair like his older sister Heather and brother Joshua. His blue eyes came from Bruce, who was still building his entrepreneurial career.

The group moved again, seeking better markets for Bruce's technology ventures where Massachusetts offered support from extended family. While Heather and Warren approached puberty, Joshua and Benjamin were still young, and Adam was the new baby. Cynthia was exhausted managing the household while her husband was frequently away.

Bruce's company, Programmer's Shop, based on catalogs of programmers for hire and software supplies, finally became a success. At its peak in the mid-1980s, the business earned one million dollars in monthly ad revenue alone, lifting the family from post-college poverty.

During this period, which should have felt like triumph, Bruce's mother, Rosamond ("Grammy Roz"), fell ill with lung cancer and passed away. The father was challenged to balanced grief with running the business and supporting the growing household which left the coming years full of trials for the couple and their expanding family. Yet, they continued forging ahead, guided by determination.

Finally, Cynthia, newly with child again, happily announced in her semi-annual newsletter to all, "Dear loved ones, we are proud to announce that our family finally will have a caboose!"

XI: APPARITION

It was on October 13, a Sunday morning at 4:29, when Rachael Edith was born into the world.

The theme song from the original Superman movies played in the background as the seasoned mother looked beyond the foot of her hospital bed. Through bay windows, she saw thousands of tiny stars sparkling in the early morning hours of the night.

Cynthia was amazed to see her premonitions fulfilled by this little girl. Her dreamwalk, bringing in the reality of having her six children, seemed a blessing come true. The artist felt she had generated her full opus.

***

After the unusually speedy return home from labor, the seasoned child-bearer sat down and swung in her large, dark rocking chair — the piece inherited from Cynthia's grandmother, Angelina Silva. Its backrest held grand carved faces at the top, with large swirling designs where her feet pushed off the ground.

Heel to tippy-toe and back again, she rocked in a balanced, meditative motion. She had cradled each of her children in that heirloom for almost ten years already. Now she was using it for the last great-grandchild she'd bring for Severino to embrace.

Glowing with contentment, remembering her dream from before, she retraced her heritage. Angelina, she imagined, would have held Edith Adelaide — her mother — and seen a face much like her own. Cynthia understood her newest born had just become the next of four generations to share precious gifts of similarity, some unseen as well.

Warren, Heather, Joshua, Benjamin, and Adam ran around their mother in the living room, circling her while she held their new little sister. Though she was only a few days old, as everyone settled to a standstill, they could see the babe's infant efforts trying to display absolute delight in existing amongst all their love.

***

By the time Rachael arrived, the family had income enough to pay for some help. Cynthia went through the trials of employing several nannies, au pair students, mother's helpers, and part-time babysitters when she and Bruce decided to separate. After growing apart, they had differences that kept them both from feeling satisfied about their lives.

In an attempt to be happier, the single mother moved her family from New England to Utah, hoping to put the Sunday school kids into good elementary schools. But her decision unraveled quickly.

Utah revealed a pecking order at the LDS church; subtle elitism that made her feel displaced as a divorced parent of so many children. With many new people in her adopted setting, she had to avoid getting lost in the noise of others telling her what was best.

A dignified matriarch, she had noble concerns for her children. She was not in competition with other families who lived only to gain more rather than simply seeking a contented life. Despite her efforts to excel as a mother, signs began to appear that the best place for her family was not where they were.

First, bullies tied up the littlest boy, Adam. He came home after his older brother, Ben, found him wrapped to a nearby tree. Then Warren went missing for some time. Beside herself, Cynthia let him back in late one evening, pleading with him because the new school had declared they'd expel him if he didn't conform.

Heather invited some girls and boys for a sleepover, but the guests tried to persuade her to worship the Devil. Her daughter told Cynthia after they had left, because she didn't want them to return.

Finally, the last straw came when the two middle boys were brought home by the local police. Their nice clothes were torn and stained.

Innocent Benjamin and Joshua, wanting to fit in with kids they had met, ended up as parties to vandalism. They had gone along while others dented mailboxes and street signs, earning a ride home from the cops who scolded them.

All of these incidents made it obvious: they were in the wrong place. Cynthia was confused — until a small thread began to shine, leading her back to her dreamquest.

One morning, she decided to take a new route to Sunday service. Curious about a recently constructed road, she let herself be guided by the unknown. The new way brought the family van to their place of worship a little earlier than usual — just enough for someone from the church to approach.

"Hello," the woman said, "I have been observing you and know in my heart that you must meet a shaman of our Navajo Tribe. I can take you after our program lets out one day."

Enough time passed for Cynthia to nearly forget, but eventually the woman appeared at her side again, ready to take her.

Manuela, the family's full-time helper, reminded Cynthia she'd bring the children home so their mother could go. That is when she met the old Navajo shaman in desert Moab.

XII: DREAMWALKER

It is in the nature of the universe to challenge things to fit, allowing us to see all the wonders of bonding.

With her wild dark hair still pulled back into an updo for church, Cynthia carried her little mini-me daughter, who's frilly little stockings matched the ribbons tied into her pigtails. They entered the shaman's house, moving through a hallway past a small bedroom and bathroom, into the kitchen, and then into the living room.

At the center was a sliding glass door, a boundary between modern life and the immortal red desert. Outside, a toddler about the same age as Cynthia's daughter sat playing.

The darling native girl wore a baby-doll brown dress over her diaper, her eyes like her grandmother's — dark and striking.

The child ran to her mother, hair flying.

Cynthia smiled, "Your granddaughter," she said. The old woman looked at the child, then at her own daughter, whose expression was unreadable.

Cynthia set her little girl down next to the other child. The girls reached out, touched hands — and both jumped back as if from a shock. They stared at each other, unmoving. The shaman smiled for the first time, watching them.

Cynthia and the elder sat. The shaman asked, "What are you here for? Or do you know?"

"I was guided by spirit to move my family," Cynthia replied.

"Well," the old woman said, "I don't have anything to tell you." A pause.

"If guided by your spirit, what does that mean to you?" The shaman finally asked.

Cynthia explained her beliefs, admitting something she thought might interest the elder more: "I am on a dreamwalk. I've asked the spiritual guides of the universe to show me what I need to know for the best outcome. When I'm unsure what to ask for, I follow these hints."

She produced a small leather pocket journal. "Anytime of day or night, I jot notes about what stirs my intuition. Later, I go back over them to translate them into a deeper storyline. It's my way of listening to the language of my soul." The shaman leaned forward. "Give me an example."

"In my dreams," Cynthia said, "I see myself drowning — water covering me, unable to breathe. Though it means so many things, I see water as emotion, so drowning means I'm overwhelmed by feelings.

I noticed I didn't try to swim. It was after my divorce. That's why I moved to Utah — to try, to surface myself. Since then, I've been finding feathers — symbols to uplift myself. These are the signs I now have seen to follow."

She continued, "For me, night dreams and waking hints are part of the same language. The process is about recognizing and following the subtle notes that resonate in the heart."

The shaman nodded, relating to the symbolism. "And how do you know what to write down?"

"It feels aligned." Cynthia said. "The right hints fit like they belong. I also cross out what's out of harmony — keeping only what sings to the heart."

The old woman stood, startling her guest.

She looked at the clock in the corner of the room before walking around the other side of her seat. There, Cynthia could see a large Native American cushion-lined stool was built like a wide box with a drawer. The shaman took a nearby sheepskin rug, placing it down before kneeling to pull the handle.

Sitting taller, Cynthia watched her host reveal several items: a large open wing, saved from a barn owl; a rattle made from what looked like a dried vegetable; several gems and stones; and a few more items that appeared like tiny warriors, vibrantly painted with bright colors, holding different tools and wearing various masks.

The Navajo woman put on a long brown coat that was very light, she would use it to shield herself from the sun. She filled her pockets with some of what she had gathered and then fit a bundle of dried juniper wood mixed with white sage into another pocket. Grabbing a matchbook, she rose to her feet, walking toward the vast outer sea of rocks and sand.

Their surroundings were almost entirely encompassed by jagged red rock, cliff edges rising tall in the distance. Gently carrying her treasures, the woman called back to Cynthia, asking her very late in motion to follow after her.

Outside, on the cement patio, was a kiddie pool and a small storage shed. Stepping into the dark red dirt, they entered an oval of stones of different sizes and colors laid carefully on the ground. Everything lay within what the easterner usually recognized as the backyard area. Cynthia speculated that the boundary must have been collected over a long time.

Unbuttoning the front of her jumper and the camisole beneath it, she felt parched as she trekked beyond the shade in her dress. The weather was dry and scorching hot. Tumbleweeds grew here and there.

Finally, the pair of women reached a far spot on a knoll, a pinnacle from which they could see the land in all directions. The New Englander worried about the heat. Why venture out to such a desolate spot? Her stockings rubbed beneath her layers.

The answer came when the Native American stopped walking. Pointing to an oval of similar stones, much smaller and barely noticeable on the ground, she told Cynthia to stand inside it. If her call to the ancestors worked, the shaman explained, a good omen would come above them.

Without knowing the purpose of the ceremony, Cynthia moved to stand inside the stones. Shading her eyes with her hands, she looked up at the cloudless sky with wonder and curiosity, while the Navajo woman lit the bundle of dried offerings. Everything ignited quickly in the hot weather.

The medicine woman softly hummed. She handed Cynthia the rattle, gesturing to use it in tune with the beat of her emotions. Chanting in her native Navajo language, the old woman lifted the owl wing, using it to blow smoke broadly in the directions she wanted it to travel. She walked around in circles, wafting the clouds down. They saw the smoke rise from their base as she sang.

With every pounding step and swing of the feathers, the shaman persuaded a whirl around them. Cynthia shook her rattle to the beat, finding herself joining the journey, deeply humming the melody.

Her eyes hazed over... She allowed them to close, feeling the air of blessings blowing around her body. The medicine woman sang louder, circling more subtly now, blowing the air ever-renewing from the burning sage.

Without conscious effort, the rattling continued while the chanting deepened with emotion. Finally, the singer began slowing down, quieting her voice. The rattle became a steady, intoxicating rhythm.

Cynthia coughed. The shaman shifted her chanting into singing louder again to bring their attention back. The student wondered if her outburst had distracted the magic. Instead of letting herself be broken in concentration, she brought herself into a state of peaceful gratitude. She relaxed her eyes again, focusing only on listening in thanks for the gifted experience.

The grace of accepting her place in life left room for something new. She was rewarded with a memory from when she was young, lying in the field on Cloudland Road. The release into true feelings brought tears welling up in her bright eyes. After so much heartache and distraction had kept her away from knowing what was correct for so long, drops of saltwater fell down Cynthia's soft cheeks—a waterfall of appreciation, longing for a time her soul felt when life was less burdened. She wanted to bring herself back to that safety, returning to her best avenue of existence.

After a while, the chanting became like a peaceful hymn. Both women lost their place in space and time. In dance, they swayed and moved. Ultimately, without knowing when, they transitioned from waking life into joined meditation.

Another jolt came to Cynthia, a feeling similar to her motherly intuition, provoking her to speak a sound—but she waited, stunned. She looked at the ground, one eye still closed tightly. The sensation reached the shaman, who also peered down. They saw their feet: one pair in Sunday shoes, the other in sandals.

Great smiles spread across their faces when they realized two other shadows. Dark silhouettes moved in and out of their boundary on the ground. The women did not break their meditative state to look at each other when they independently realized the movements below were from great birds.

Flying high in the burning sky above, two golden eagles soared.

Finally, the old woman's smile reached Cynthia for the first time as they embraced the blessing.

Upon returning to the house, they raved with delight at their discovery. Two little faces appeared in the window, transfixed. Watching their elders beaming, the children had no idea what had happened.

The two women asked if the girls noticed the birds flying around them, but their answer came silently, with wide eyes. Nevertheless, everyone enjoyed the warm affection.

Cynthia never felt more connected after what they had experienced, satisfied now that she was spiritually returned to a greater destiny. In the end, as if it were any other Sunday after church, the mother and daughter arrived home, but this time smelling of a desert ceremony.

XIII: GIFTS FROM MOAB

A few months in Utah passed. Cynthia returned several times to the medicine healer from the red rock desert, Moab. Convinced by the omen they had shared, the tribal woman told Cynthia their meeting was no coincidence — they were called to be together. A celebrated elder, she believed she could persuade the tribe to allow her to train the young mother as an apprentice.

Cynthia felt that what she knew could only be deepened by releasing the old and starting afresh. It was all part of her dreamwalk. She began making choices based on self-empowerment. It shocked her to realize how many decades had passed without her fully studying her spiritual growth. Feeling steadied again, she vowed to follow her own translation of life, allowing nothing to distract her.

Instead of remarrying, as her mother had, she committed herself to her children, her life, her art. Though she had not yet chosen it, Cynthia knew she would adopt a new last name — unique, self-chosen, and filled with the wisdom of an artist of the universe.

Soon, she sensed it was time to return to the East Coast. A few following weeks of quiet to recenter herself had strengthened her resolve. Each day she visited her new Navajo friend, the elder allowed no frivolous thought.

Cynthia already knew where to go from the vision she had during her first ceremony. Though the shaman wished her to stay, by their third meeting there was an understanding.

Gifts were gathered and given, with prayers for a blessed future. For the young mother, the medicine woman bequeathed a piece of her ceremonial juniper wood, tucked with meaningful stones into a handmade satchel of rabbit leather.

Before Cynthia could leave, the elder picked up a gold-wrapped fossilized shark tooth adorned with turquoise and an Atlantic pearl bound in gold wire. She explained each element in detail before placing it in Cynthia's hands. Then she turned to Cynthia's child.

Over Rachael Edith's small neck, newly three years old, she placed a hand-beaded necklace — layers of white beads with a fringed centerpiece bearing an eagle's head. The little girl's hands played with her new treasure as the shaman added another single thread of light-blue beads.

"Blue symbolizes distinction," the elder said, fastening the clasp, "and the eagle represents the type of spiritual strength she will carry — to see from far away and pursue with fierce precision."

The woman rested her hand on the girl's forehead, reciting a Navajo blessing in her native tongue. Quieted by the deep aura in the room, Rachael closed her eyes. A smile spread across her face when she reopened them, striking the room with a shared moment of appreciation. They embraced under the small desert house's threshold as tears fell softly to the earth.

Leaving was difficult for everyone. To sooth the upcoming trip, Cynthia decided she had enough for a family astrology reading. She gave the astrologer each child's birth time, place, and date. The reading ended with Rachael.

The astrologer told Cynthia her youngest had more of the underworld in her chart than usual and should be surrounded by plants and animals for her best life. That lingered in Cynthia's mind. She realized she must return to where she had last been in harmony.

The desert vision renewed in her thoughts — a vision of rolling Vermont hills and farms — and she took it as a good omen.

The mother bought her first new van, a gray Mazda with a black stripe, and filled it with her children, toys, activity books, and food. Only eight months after moving from Massachusetts to Utah, Cynthia packed a U-Haul and headed back East. Her mother Edith's husband, Morry, drove the truck behind them.

The children sang on the road, at first pleasantly, then intentionally off-key to irritate the driver. Benjamin, carsick like clockwork, grossly filled potato chip bags along the way.

After four nights in hotels, they arrived in snow-covered Woodstock, Vermont, where Cynthia had rented a six-bedroom colonial.

A blizzard was passing through, leaving three feet of powder. The house was huge and freezing, so that first night they slept in the living room in sleeping bags, Morry layed down a new carpet Cynthia had purchased on the way, spreading it out before the fire.

In the early days, Heather and Warren urged their mother to return to Hingham, Massachusetts, where they had friends. But Cynthia waited, following her dreamwalking promise to hold out for the right home.

When an estate came up for sale in Pomfret the next summer, she went to see it. Built into a hollow at the juncture of Cloudland Road and Galaxy Hill Road, it felt just right. She renovated it to her heart's desire, moving in with her "little chickies" in spring, just as she turned forty.

Pomfret Springs Farm came with a giant red barn in the valley — and to everyone's delight, Big Kitty, the half-wild tomcat from their rental, somehow found them there.

The move marked the start of their new life.

Though they settled well, unlike before, they stopped attending church by their second Christmas in Vermont. When a local pastor told Cynthia she was bound for hell for believing in dreamwalking, she replied, "If that's true, I hope it's warmer there."

Knowing she had spent decades driving them dutifully to worship each Sunday previously, now their mother was content to let her children choose their own paths forward.

XIV: RECOLLECTION – GIVEN TO PAUSE

Every bit of turning to adventure brings reason for coloring more until passing beyond the unknown, completely reaching what manifested; epiphany unveiled in the exit.

Flora and fauna sing, affecting my senses while I unravel meanings from dreams and reality now.

At one point in my labyrinth of labyrinths, I see myself within an enchanted region of a greater quest. My eternal journey has curved and weaved as my soul grew steadily, with no clear finish line for so long that this resting point in my list of recollections is a wonder to me.

In this special place, a babbling river erupted from a natural spring. The contents bubbled up from the depths of the earth, spraying life-giving water. A variety of edible perennials was growing in the microsphere. They surrounded a large, untouched area made of moss, which carpeted a clearing in the wood, altogether forming an enchanted opening. Here was one of those places where mother earth is soaked in treasures, and a person could get lost for hours feeling her riches—so I did.

I chose to seat myself upon a small, unique wooden bench, noticing its intricate construction, befitting for it to earn its residency amongst the divine. A skilled artisan hand-carved the exquisite work of art to fit precisely into a natural boulder of rose quartz. It was a balance of dark hardwood mixed with contrasting light softwood within the arrangement, making it all a masterpiece, charming with natural colors chosen from the edges of the trail leading to it. One armrest had intricate floral designs, and the rest was carved with geometric patterns, appearing as if several artists had contributed their mediumship of beauty into this one place to sit.

Behind me, facing away as I came to sit upon the throne, stood a bronze statue of an egret. With its long neck, the elegant, tall bird had aged to its natural green patina. In my collapsed state, the figure was aligned with my crown chakra, frozen in action. Based upon perspective, the bird was either lifting its wings to take flight or flaring them down in landing.

Quietly seated back-to-back with the effigy epitomized by flight, I slowed my consciousness into meditation, an inkling telling me to reward myself through studying the icon's artistry further in spirit. After some time, something which resembled the presence of Sundara prompted me to awaken. My eyes opened directly toward my armrest. There, I noticed a notch handle opening to a small cupboard. Inside was a jade bowl I could remove—a secret gift, easily overlooked had I not given myself to a moment of pause.

Laid within the bowl were handmade leather pouches of herbs and one dark, rough piece of black stone. The small sacks had lavender, sage, chamomile, rose hip, and thyme—the poetry of it all truly enhancing my vantage point. My heart was overfilled, witnessing the grace seeping through the ambiance I was enjoying. Taking out the bowl, I filled it with water from the spring before adding bits of the lavender and chamomile. The sun made a warm tea, which I sipped, prolonging the enjoyment of a restful period.

Turning my body into a new position upon this grand cathedral, I fell asleep. While awakening, I realized I was fondling the dark little piece of stone in my hand. Without thought, I rose to my feet. Movement brought change to my perspective. I felt most compelled to walk toward the flowers that surrounded me. Venturing toward loveliness kept me dazed, eventually following the edge of life until my alignment arranged me near the statue.

The bird was so tiny when imagining it behind my shoulder-blades. Now I found its wings were larger than the grand bench had been, its head somehow harmonized again with my own as I stood. I found myself empowered next to it. Looking back to see the armchair in my past but peering further at the egret's details, I noticed others who must have come here like myself had struck marks upon its base.

Holding the stone in my hand, I reflected on its unusual light weight. With thoughts on my newest revelation, I reached down, gathering some dried roughage to place under where I would strike the metal. In an instant, the flint sparked enough to light what I'd constructed. I added some small sticks to feed the flame before using it more. It felt good to burn part of the sage from the seat I had arisen, wafting the smoke all around in a dance with my spirit.

After my secret performance, before replacing the bowl to its home within the elegant armrest, I took the thyme and added it to another sun-warmed drink, stoking my fire, requiring further peace before my departure. It was necessary for me to enjoy contemplating the whole of my pilgrimage the same way I had pictured my next steps using these fantastic gifts. Etiquette dictated I braid some treasured copper which I had within my pocket, making a button to wrap the strings of the pouch around, closing it more beautifully now.

Opening the floral-carved armrest to replace the items I had now adorned with my own touch revealed an engraving under the lid I hadn't noticed before. Balancing myself quietly within harmony led me to see it. The image was within a square border, carved to look like a sun drifting from its upper right corner back into view, rays reaching diagonally across to the bottom left. I recognized the symbol was from my favorite artist; Sundara had left her signature! Though I'd seen it several times before, it came to me now that maybe her symbol was, in fact, an eye. Without its top lid, it is all-seeing, with the bottom lashes striking through the frame. I couldn't know for sure, but recalled her teaching, "Whatever pleases the spirit must carry some truth." So it was.

Upon preparing to go, it became clear that I had not looked around enough before this place. I wondered how the unexpected turns and the many ways of perceiving everything had distracted me from the whole, making the lengthy path all the more seemingly endless until I had the mind to be more present.

Indeed, I had not organized myself to share anything much, revealed by those before me. How long had I just walked, lacking mindfulness of the now, only with a mind toward what might be next?

Sundara was my ultimate heroine for having awakened first. Humbled, all became clear with the powerful emotions of my impending exit from this great midpoint. Finding myself enlightened with the importance of breaking those patterns, I preserved my lesson deeply into my soul. Slowly, I carried myself in a different way over several ages to find more momentary enjoyment through times of pause.

As I walked on, I knew I must have been catatonic in the beginning stage, rushing through decades, possibly centuries of lifetimes with little gained. Through my exit, a rush of wisdom came. I realized an existence where each step along my dream quest could be felt like an entire lifetime. Finally, rather than simply traversing the trails of living, I was compelled to begin creating more meaningful gifts of gratitude to leave behind. Through my blind faith in this new direction, with no clear view of how it happened, I came to learn what was needed to allow my spiritual being to exist at a higher level.

Remaining ever stalwart, I am brought back to my current self now as I continue observing the web of movements, centers, and endless designs coming together. This pattern reaches through time and space so much that any one part of it seems nothing in comparison to the whole of my existence. Once attaining the awareness of eternity, seeing how endings were centers which were also beginnings, I notice currently how much less the disappointments, carried in my soul's short episodes on earth, affect my everlasting emotional being.

My newfound awareness brings grateful endurance into my fortitude for living. Feeling as if a part of time itself, any pains now compare little to all I could go through in multiple existences. Wiser in my exit from that mystical site, I finally came to my own ruling.

XV: SPIRITUAL COLLAGE

On a bright morning in 1991, Cynthia spread several well-loved *National Geographic* magazines across her desk. She was drawn to create a collage — a spiritual portrait made of images and symbols that would speak to her through the language of dreamwalking.

At the center of her creation, she placed a striking woman in a magnificent shawl, her hair adorned with feathers, an everlasting flame held in her palm. Beneath this towering figure, she arranged rows of tiny people reaching toward her sandaled feet, as if calling for her light. The finished image seemed alive — a scene of guidance and devotion.

Rachael leaned against the side of her mother's desk, watching with fascination. When Cynthia ended, she handed her daughter a fresh sheet of white paper.

"Make your own," she said, smiling. "Tear out and arrange the images that give you a feeling of joy. Don't worry about ruining the magazines, they're meant to be used."

The room was warm with the smell of paper and paste. Magazines were scattered across the carpet in front of the dormant fireplace.

Rachael flipped through the glossy pages, eyes catching on colors and shapes. She began tearing, gluing, arranging some images large and commanding, others small and tucked into corners. The quiet scratch of tearing paper mixed with the occasional thump of a magazine falling to the floor.

Cynthia left the room to give her daughter space, but she could hear the focused energy of the work. She knew this was more than an art project; it was Rachael's first experience of translating her subconscious into a map of symbols.

When Cynthia returned, she felt the hum of meaning in the collage. She recognized it instantly: the same pull she felt when she was guided to gather dream signs into her journal.

She had taught herself, and now was teaching her child, that dreamwalking could happen with scissors and glue just as easily as in sleep or life. The process was the same:

One: gather what stirs you, without judging it. Two: arrange it until it feels right. Three: step back, notice patterns, and read them like a story of symbolisms.

Cynthia knelt beside Rachael and studied the piece. She pointed out a curious detail — the way most of the faces in the collage seemed to be looking in the same direction. Her finger traced their gaze across the page, noting how arrow-shaped objects pointed the same way.

"You see how the energy flows here?" she asked. "That tells us there's movement in your story. It is a journey."

At the bottom center lay a white lamb, its little pink nose nestled in the grass beneath a great tree.

"In some languages, 'Rachel' means 'little ewe,'" Cynthia said. "See how she's curled in safety? That's you."

Beside the tree stood a massive stone foot in a sandal, part of a robed statue crowned with grapevines. One arm pressed against his chest, the other outstretched toward the opposite side of the page.

"He's pointing you somewhere," Cynthia murmured.

Her eyes followed the line of the statue's arm to a roaring waterfall that filled the center of the collage.

"Water," she explained, "is the deepest conductor of emotion. This waterfall is power but also a test. One day, something will feel this big, this overwhelming. You'll think you have no choice but to fall into it."

She paused, touching her daughter's arm.

"But you do have a choice. See how the statue's arm creates a path above the water? It's telling you there is always a way to rise without sinking."

Above the falls stretched a distant mountain range. And on its ridge, almost hidden in shadow, stood the black silhouette of a large cat.

"A catamount," Cynthia said softly. "A creature that walks the edge between earth and sky. That's where you'll find yourself once you cross the challenge. The cat's energy — independence, strength, precision — will be yours."

The two of them studied the page together. For each image, Cynthia showed her how to ask: Why this? Why now? and to trust the answers that rose from inside.

By the time they finished, Rachael wasn't just holding a collage, she was holding her first symbolic map. She had learned, without yet realizing it, how to listen to the language of images and see her life through signs.

Later, as they carried a vase of flowers and a light lunch to the porch overlooking the brook, Rachael asked, "Will I know if it all comes true?"

"Only time will tell, my darling girl," *Sundara* replied.

XVI: RECOLLECTION – THE SEA CLIFF

I see myself again. My balanced walk comes into harmony with the petite and graceful strides of someone else. Our hands clasp together as we embrace.

It is Sundara! We had spun away but now turn toward each other again. Spiraling around, we savor our deep connection.

After swinging in opposite directions, we have returned to our old tree, now grown to great magnitude and surrounded by an oasis. We rest beneath its young and elder branches, wiser with experience and taking pause more seriously, allowing this part of our journey to rejuvenate us.

Together, we stand before the familiar cliff leading down to the sea—where every passage must either end or dare to transform. We listen to the ocean's crash followed by peaceful silence, the water rekindling our many memories. The hypnotic drumming of the waves repeats the waxing and waning of existence.

Although separate in our growth during the previous life, our souls have been drawn back to each other—like the sea, nothing can hold back a wave when behind it comes the force of an entire ocean.

Under the grand branches, our songs merge into a duet. Surprised, we see our presence from the past etched into stone—Sundara's artwork fossilized in the ground. Long ago, when spirit was better known in waking life, she created designs from vibrations of gratitude. Those engravings now remain as proof of what was, and of the lifetimes in which we regenerated together.

When we converge, a familiar spark ignites—a reincarnation opening into new levels each time. We recall the number of times we've met, our joy undiminished by whether we know the exact count. We have been born in many forms—often women, sometimes men—often finding each other as family or friends.

In this recollection, Sundara begins to believe her art could be shared beyond us, as a thread of life carrying spiritual uplift from the universe into something tangible. I would become part of what flowed through her, lifetime after lifetime, until a barrier grew in the world—a wedge between beings and the healing earth.

Still, barefoot under the mother trees, we remember. Nature sings for us not to forget what will save us.

Above, day-blind stars shine as we string together our lifetimes beneath their ever-present light.

XVII: RECOLLECTION – EGYPT

The previous recollection rushes into the next.

Parts of my skin peek from under a lengthy covering draping over me. Golden, tanned, adorned with artistic anklets and toe rings, I realize this is not my current body.

In this memory, centuries from now, I feel tall as I step onto a stone staircase. I am a woman again, noticing several rings around my graceful fingers, bracelets bangle around my wrists as I lift my dress to climb.

The enchantment continues with the richness of my regalia, embroidered in detail, falling over me with openings at my hips and down my back. My ensemble flows freely, revealing tattoos from underarm to above the knee, symbols I cannot recall in detail. Earrings clasp my ears, a charm shifts on my forehead as I bend, three straight arm bands embrace my upper left arm, two more around my right forearm, all hand-pounded dark gold.

The present has never been so alive in my recollections. As I climb into the giant sandstone building, part of this woman remains strong in my spirit. It takes a moment to absorb what I remember of being her.

I approach a tremendous crowd. Sensing their silent gaze, I reach the top of the staircase, passing beneath opulent front columns. A few others follow me; they are in my service. My direction is toward family. Trained to carry myself taller than the doorways, I feel small among the stands where they sit. Understanding dawns as I rest beside my elders, forefront of everyone.

In the desert heat, cooled by the structure's shade, I recognize a memory of being gifted more than I could balance. It brings clarity to the truth of what I did, which took it all away.

***

Sundara had placed herself to provide a life where she could love and uplift, using me to bring creations of architecture to the world, each a venue for her talents. I made a grand impact implementing her plans in my name.

The episode boded well for both my progression and hers. Yet patience and humility did not last in me. Though holding great luck, until desires manifested in the world, our soul's connection remained fragile.

My dear soul companion, Sundara, was my grandfather this lifetime, keen to let things be, providing within prescribed boundaries. Foolishly, I sought greater impact, forsaking my dreamquest. Self-centered, I made myself more important than being guided.

Even with our divine partnership, creation as leaders wasn't enough. I was an addict of change. That was my downfall. I compared everyone to Sundara and me, seeing others as forgetting their own ability to dreamwalk. That lifetime now remains powerful in memory.

My clear conscience revealed a future where love could shine through the universe. Handling such destiny alone was impossible. Directing my vision toward the masses, regardless of their understanding, was foolish. Radicalized, I gave speeches about bettering all, forcing dialogue. My efforts were juvenile; my connection to the Great All was egotistical and short-sighted.

Thinking I could progress, I strayed from true north. Using my position to govern rather than wait, I was mistaken. Ironically, my soul turned to face my own scale of justice.

Disappointed, impatience grew. I made a rash choice: to chastise myself, hopping off that thread of existence to somewhere else. Self-sacrifice, thinking it advanced me, further broke my strand of purpose. A martyr, I believed giving my luck showed wisdom. Having lived spiritually free in unique social rank with Sundara, I swore not to return to similar folly.

Spoiled with blessings I took for granted, the rush of lessons was inevitable. Humility and challenge balanced me again. Arrogantly, I had pushed myself for personal review, swelling with embarrassment.

Perhaps I was meant to live that fortunate position to teach embracing blessings and using them for good. Instead, I was lost in digressions, unaware of letting the universe conduct the tone and tune of truest life. My purpose was simple: follow Sundara, be drawn to her, never anywhere but the best way. Yet I ended that life on a tangent, tipping away from alignment.

Returned to the ether, I lost my way, farther from my cosmic function. Ultimately, for the cosmos to teach appreciation and servility, the Great All preserved what we had gained before flinging me in a new direction.

***

Straying from my guided path was dangerous. I could not pause; I had ordered my own lessons. Penitence became my path back to Sundara. Dirt-floor living and challenges kept me from awakening for many short lives.

Impoverished times left deep scars. Thoughts of wanting life's necessities distracted me, questioning why I felt divine yet trapped. Age did not matter; I had made a youthful mistake. How I flung myself from where I was, and how I could return, was my new query.

I had to lose all direction, letting my dreamquest guide me. Yet seeking simple freedoms, I forgot to give myself space to heed my soul's call.

One pivotal lifetime sticks forever: kept in darkness without windows, my soul knew more existed. Excruciating emotional torture led me into slight mental lunacy, until I realized if I could not go physically, I could ask my spirit the way.

Desperate for peace, I let go. Lying down my suffering body, I surrendered. My last breaths, noticed within my mind, finally freed my soul.

Between that life and the next, I awoke. Exhausted, my spirit recalled quiet relief from lighter existence. Floating in ether, I patiently felt cradled within universal love. I was freed.

***

Sundara, sensing my absence, departed Egypt. Her last lifetime there was quaint, perfect for any aligned angel, yet she felt something wrong without my closeness. Through change, she knew we could return to each other.

Hooking the thread of her heart with mine into prolonged transcendence, she paused in bliss until I freed myself from confusion. She held through millennia, awaiting my corrected alignment. Once clear of my location, she hurried to regain momentum, birth importance.

A powerful sovereign in spirit, Sundara transformed into an heiress, born to a maiden whose virginity was gifted to raise her family's status. Guided only by our prior connection and my location, she acted—but karmic repayment remained. Self-directed choices meant we were challenged, losing sight of our connection once again.

In that new life, we started unrecognizable, cousins ignorant of our true relationship, facing blind faith. Proving our deserving connection promised the reward of timeless harmony.

Creating Beauty's art became secondary; her responsibilities were too great. Choosing self over providence led to restricted life, testing remembrance of what was forgotten.

XVIII: EMERLYE ARTS BEGINS

Cynthia needed to take a trip. She asked her boys to make sure their baby sister got on the bus in the morning. Then, at about 9 a.m., Rachael woke up alone, upstairs in their old creaky farmhouse.

Tears began to run down the little girl's face as she realized she was by herself. To find comfort, she went to look at family photos. She was deeply worried that her mother might, somehow, never, ever come home.

The girl gathered as many pictures as she could into a heap around her before deciding to go outdoors. In a sudden flash, Rachael saw herself summoning her large gray and black striped tabby cat who, in the image, would come from a walk around the corner. Aware that the cat had not been seen by anyone for several days now, she ventured outside uncertain about what she might find.

Confident in his freedom, the family had allowed the kitty to enjoy an unrestricted life with a stable home to return to whenever he wished. Cynthia would often say, as others had, "Ahh, to be a cat."

Hoping to find comfort with a friend, the girl called out with all her might, "Kitty! Here, Kitty!"

Sobbing, eyes fuzzy, she walked toward the more dangerous part of the property.

The road through the middle of their farm was a forty-five-mile-an-hour speed zone. It was dangerous for children. Rachael's eyes continued to fog with tears. Intending to cross toward the barn, she kept looking for the cat, who she hoped was possibly on the other side.

As she moved without caution, closer to the giant white fence opening to the driveway, she was past the point of safety, determined to move forward, approaching the speeding cars.

Just before she reached the center yellow lines of the roadway, she felt a change in the air around her. Attuned to ancient parts of herself, her adolescent fit of sadness suddenly felt ridiculous.

Wiping her eyes to look around, she noticed spring flowers blooming back where she had come from safely. Less inclined to go where it frightened her, she called once more, doubting the intuitive feeling she had that everything would be all right, somehow, if she just returned to bed.

The not-really-abandoned young girl felt confused as she was not tired at all. She desperately hoped her furry friend would come for what she proclaimed was her greatest time of need, at almost seven years old.

When a final call did not summon him, she slowly turned around inside the fence, ignoring the loud sounds of a car zooming past.

As she made her steps up the driveway incline, she noticed an ant crawling slowly toward the house. A fantasy started in the girl's imagination that here was a different friend!

The child crouched to pick up the insect. Assuming it wanted to go where she wanted to go, she sped up their journey together.

Sillily chasing the bug, trying not to smoosh it as it raced from her fingers, suddenly, there was the cat!

Just as she'd seen in her first inkling of what to do with herself to find comfort earlier, Big Kitty appeared around the corner of the white fence, coming from the road to sit at her little bare feet. Still standing in her nightgown, the child's eyes noticed him the same way the ant drew her attention toward life's intricate movements.

The strong, tough father cat seemed glad for the attention. He must have heard the singing calls for him. Calmed by his presence, forgetting the tiny ant, Rachael leaned down, lifting him up.

Big as he was in her little arms, she awkwardly carried him up the long driveway. The cat didn't always allow the child to carry him in her small arms because she was too young to hold him properly but, this time, he remained patient.

The girl brought him into the library room where the fireplace was cold and unlit. She could snuggle with him there on her mother's light-colored special couch, where no one was supposed to ever sit, feeling the rays of the sun reaching in toward them as the morning furthered into the afternoon. As if being bad would bring her attention, she liked knowing Cynthia would surely find her there, even if she rested her eyes.

When young Rachael placed the big tabby cat on the couch, the wise old father cat immediately laid himself down, purring extra loudly. Innocently, the girl showed him the photos of her mom, the ones she had collected into a pile earlier. Big Kitty rubbed his whiskered cheek on the picture frames. Within a short time, under his guard, she fell asleep.

Cynthia came home eventually, as she always did, and all was right again. What nobody knew was that the single mother had made a drive down to Boston that night before. It was a two-and-a-half-hour trek which she made willingly for Warren, who was in trouble at a difficult point in his life down there, attending private school. Her memory of his exhausting past rang in her mind as she drove.

As a kid, he was banned from preschool for his mischievousness. After that, he was kicked out of multiple elementary schools, both public and private. Finally, he was enrolled in an academy for advanced children. He flourished there, receiving the attention needed to occupy his overstimulated brain and keep him out of trouble.

That school was great for him until the family had to move, which put him back into public schools where he was expelled again.

Cynthia understood Warren was bored and neglected as a genius, and this factor was causing a rift at home. The mother of six saw that he would constantly stir up his five younger siblings.

The fact was, messing with his siblings proved to be a great source of entertainment for the eldest, though it undermined his mother's authority. It was for this reason Cynthia had sent Bruce Warren Jr. to room and board elsewhere at the time the rest of the family arrived to live in Vermont.

This time, the teenager had been playing with friends in the hallways of his new academy, throwing a football back and forth after hours, when another kid threw him the ball. In his attempt to catch it, he crashed through a door.

When the glass broke, his wrist and left arm took the brunt of the impact. Some shards cut into his skin badly.

The accident set off the building's safety alarms. Fire trucks and ambulances came, turning the incident into a much larger, expensive fiasco.

Reviewing his long record of expulsions, the headmaster told his mother her son could not return to that school after the hospital.

Cynthia stayed in the emergency ward that night, answering questions from surgeons about Warren's health. They were concerned about whether they could save all the movement in his wrist and hand. Cynthia was distraught but still had to consider her other children. He had increasingly tested her ability to choose what was right for the whole family over each person individually.

Indeed, she had made up her mind to continue to separate Warren from country life because of his constant misconduct. But what hurt her most was knowing her son was not bad or evil enough to deserve such severe punishment. Instead, he was caught in his own intelligence, too young to see the purpose of learning self-control and stuck without the attention he needed.

When Cynthia got the hospital call, she packed something to do. Usually, she read books for entertainment, but this time she chose to meditate, seeking a better answer for her son in the way she'd found her direction dreamwalking.

Heather, Joshua, and Benjamin were mature enough to babysit overnight for Adam and Rachael, but Cynthia still remained worried with five children at home, hours away.

The artist grabbed some art supplies before she left. She had lost what helped her feel very creative with traditional art since living in Holyoke. While there with Bruce, she had produced a gallery show that completely sold out.

Selling all her work had made her very proud, but her life as a childbearing wife to her new husband after graduating had been too busy for her to continue. Now, years later, she realized she had a new, quiet life in an artisanal state where life as an artist would well suit her surroundings. All these years later, she took her chance to create again.

While Warren was in surgery, Cynthia thought deeply about what to do. She drew a spiritual image with her colored pencils. The drawing had a warm feeling with lots of blues and yellows. It became an angelic figure, its bright aura radiating around its edges.

The heavenly figure she drew was like a guardian angel she felt nearby. She was upset, and this illustration offered comfort and guidance.

The angel became the first drawing for *Emerlye Arts*. Cynthia strengthened her unique talent for decades after, always remembering that premier angel was born from her eldest child's calamity. It had come to her at a time when there was nothing more to do than follow Beauty's immortal thread of love from the universe.

XIX: RECOLLECTION - REUNITED

In shared laughter we move the physical into a tune that is greater than ourselves separately, the divine alignment bringing joy into our hearts, coaxing us to move forward whichever way will continue the rush of advancement.

A young teenage girl dressed in elegant clothes sits in a carriage, pulled by four dappled gray horses. The grand animal's magnificent long tails full of curly hair swish in front of the driver.

The carriage is seen coasting along with dark mahogany edges curving around its creamy-white shiny sides. The tack worn by each horse matches the hardware they pull, all contrasting dark brown leather with polished brass, shining like gold when moving, turning to and fro around each winding corner in the road.

The elegant, cream-colored ride rolled in from the Southeast where Sundara and her two children reside. They have returned to their country estate for a weekend picnic on the coast.

Another woman sitting beside her seems to be a handmaiden for the young lady. Sundara asks if she would please open the window to let the warm summer breeze flow through the cabin.

Today the ride carries them away from duty and responsibility. The bumpy road has many turns and hills, alongside manicured patches of greenery. The driver can't quite see the girl hidden around the bend ahead, her fancy shoes dangling loosely, while she sits, awaiting them.

I am that girl. In this lifetime, I learn how to be alone without being lonely; my connection with my ultimate self is with me, comforting me. I retain my patience, allowing what is to come to manifest its best possible outcome.

Although neither of us can realize the extent yet, my connection with my cousin in this lifetime is very special. I am ecstatic to have been born again into a good life, distinctly remembering my appreciation for it very much.

Within the memory, my shoes barely fasten onto my feet. I wear delicate stockings with traditional, slip-on day heels. They are light pink and intricately embroidered to harmonize with the rest of my attire. Obviously specially made for someone not planning to get dirty.

I am sitting on a stone wall, by a grassy slope, nearby a stream. My dress has layers of light colored, floral patterns under a solid crimson bodice. Creamy lace on my undergarments shows when I lift my dress to get a better look at my shoes.

The landscape is full of rolling hills that have patches of forest. Brooks and streams weave all around. Everything in sight from this spot seems manicured; meticulously tamed by endless efforts to contain the wild wilderness, which I know well from previous explorations.

Gazing toward the clouds, with the sudden hope that I may have just glimpsed a rainbow. I turn so quickly; my weight becomes unbalanced. I kick, forgetting my pretty heels. While shifting my attention away from them, I lose one. In reaction, my hand raises to my mouth.

I quickly reach down to take off the other heel and remove my stockings before I hop off the wall into the uncut grassy slope in my bare feet. Everything creates a whoosh of air. My garments whiffing and fluffing like deserts of all kinds in many delicious flavors when I spring from the stone embankment without planning my landing and inadvertently fall.

Tumbling became, while attempting to rescue the lost shoe, I was amused, laughing at my silly accident. Soon after, the uncontrollable silliness wobbled my grabbing hand with more giggles, further impeding the retrieval of the lost shoe, it rolls away from me more even as I drop to my hands and knees to get a better grasp.

Finally, I save the fancy foot covering at the edge of the gurgling water. As I rose, the stone I balanced my footing on shifted. The jolts which came, result in me flinging the rosy shoe somewhere else, again!

Looking back toward the road, I assume it went into a nearby bush. With the other heeled slipper sticking out of a large secret pocket I recently sewed into my skirt, I walk from the ragged edges of the brook. Not stopping my chuckles, I reached my mischievous shoe again.

Although my training and etiquette tell me never to sit on the ground, I resolved to cast those silly rules to the wind already that day when I had tumbled down the embankment. Seating myself into the tall unkempt grassy roadside, I looked forward across the water, seeing two squirrels climbing about the trees in front of me.

With a smile of gratitude for life's tiny pleasures and realizing the luxury of my innocent existence, my soul beams with the love for being alive. Cautious, I knew somehow, I was finally free from my past.

I looked again at my pretty white, suede gloves hanging from the sleeves of my overcoat which was still draping on the wall. They were blowing in the wind like flags. There is a soft eggshell-color decorating the silk lining interior of my long, leather coat, matching also with the side hat clipped in my hair.

The same colors from my dress and coat flow into the embroidery on my rosy colored shoes. Every garment boasts the most intricate, beautiful stitching which I had proudly sewn myself. The details render my entire outfit to be multi-colored with harmony.

I begin to pick a bundle of wild flowers. On this day, I wait for Sundara, the one who is also looking forward to meeting me. She is unrealized within our greater legacy, but so am I.

A sweet peacefulness reigns in the center of this daily labyrinth where I chase my runaway fancy slipper. I am simply guided to know there is more. To my delight, what had sparked before all the recent suffering was now rekindled in me; the ability to align to my lessons spiritually and become renewed.

Now, crouched from view below the edge of the stone wall, I am content to remain seated in the grass. I smile under the rays of the sun until a sound reaches me from the wheels of a carriage stopping.

Apparently, Sundara first noticed some excitement when earlier I had flung my pink shoe high into the air. I must have been beside the noisy water when she had turned the corner, nearing where I was. My friend arrived before I noticed the familiar sound beyond the rapids. I know she sees me, her cousin. Laughing, she questions, "What are you doing down there?"

Suddenly, I remember the constraints of status and considerable rank. The laughter had come from a place inside us where we knew true freedom, a relaxed comfort beyond culture and present-day traditions.

My cousin and I had both determined, no spiritual advancement would come from fighting against obscure obstacles. Indeed, stress from trying to meet social demands would eventually render itself pointless in time.

I stood up, whirling my coat around me, uncovering my stockings which I had previously tucked into the stone wall before hunting my other items. My toes still uncovered; I was making more of an effort to connect before the carriage disappeared. "Pick up those stockings and put them back on at once!" the strict companion instructed me before prompting Sundara next to her. "We really must reach the estate so that I can prepare your bath prior to retiring for the evening, your Eminence."

I looked down at my stockings tucked into a crack between two boulders and quickly grabbed them. They went nicely into my dress pockets, next to my shoes. Stubbornly, my feet would not be restricted as I walked barefoot because, indeed, one of my favorite pastimes was to enjoy the lush green grass growing on the side of the lane as it tickled between my toes.

The princess, her maid and her two children continued to their landing by the sea. They set off to resume traveling down the road again, but behind the back of madam strictness, the smirks on our faces shared vibes much larger than what showed upon each of our lips.

Simultaneously returning to the residence, we arrived. As the visitors parked, I stole up to my chambers having already moved there in the spring.

I was quick to dress more appropriately. Mindful of the rules of being seen and not heard, I pondered the day's revelations, thinking, one day, I might discover how to have the things around me in my life reflect who I am more exactly.

As that lifetime progressed, Sundara and I continued forward on our own, embracing our connection. We came to perceive life as a great game to succeed while others thought we should be serious, observing as we expressed our spiritual energy.

I recall the curious feeling of waiting for the best times to happen inevitably. She and I knew that the entire free world would never be able to adhere to minority desires for controlling the timelines of such major events as a great spiritual awakening. After all, like the ocean which covers over most of our land body, the world we know is constantly in flux with a powerful flowing of fate.

Inevitably, reversion to the way we evolved for eons prior to disconnection, we felt in touch with our spiritual heritage, somehow predicting it was returning at a massive scale.

Our efforts to remain playful did lead the two of us with love back toward our destiny in the end, as it would prove to do so for everyone.

XX: RECOLLECTION – IMMORTAL BOND

Great big boats knocked together, floating in the harbor. Bound by their ties, they lay still for months until called into use. Yet forever, with their unique sails and colors, all the vessels ride the same ocean's surface. The water remains constant, weaving around the globe beneath them.

I recall the port felt out of place, though the countryside stirred familiarity, and the ocean's calm was soothing. I was happy living a life where I could participate in my husband's family business on cargo ships, even while knowing the constraints on women clashed with my adventurous spirit.

By the time I rejoined my soul comrade, I had fully resubmerged into my dreamquest, joyfully exploring new depths of living, shedding distractions so that the familiar love between us could flourish.

Born again in this life, my gentle father named me something unusual for the time. He and my mother let me play with my brothers and encouraged me to read, write, swim, and more—nurturing my independence, uncommon for a daughter then.

On a brisk September day, I was organizing reports from the foreman as my crew packed our family's ships. My husband had allowed me to lead groups of men in and out of the harbor for his business. Somehow, I had persuaded him and his relatives that I was suited for this 'man's job.'

The efficiency I brought transformed the chaotic shipyard system. I was proud —until my abilities, unusual for a woman at that time, sparked suspicion. Nonsense! I knew that strict schedules would prove transparency, yet fear lingered that my work might end abruptly, only instead to be given to a man.

That morning, as I studied new symbol-filled, color-coded checklists, laughter erupted. The voice commanding attention belonged to the Queen. Scurrying down, I bowed and stood ready to serve.

Freezing into a curtsy, a thought startled me: this might be the moment I lose all my freedoms. The Queen was laughing at me! That couldn't be good.

Her regal carriage rolled nearby. She had come, driven by rumors of my organizational skill, demanding to meet a woman other than herself capable of commanding a sizable army of men. I wondered how to earn her trust.

The Queen motioned for me to rise. Our eyes met in silence. It was not sight, but feeling. Looking into hers, I recognized a familiar kinship—awareness of my dearly beloved returned.

She asked how many men answered to me. "Seventy-two, Your Highness." I lowered my gaze, curious if she knew me. Surrounded by her entourage, I held back further words.

"Do your men often defy you?" she asked. "Not once, my Queen," I replied. An awkward silence followed.

"I am my husband's humble messenger. His family owns this fleet, and I organize their shipments." She smirked, squinting as I averted my eyes.

Transfixed, I recognized my superior as Sundara—my recent cousin and ancient connection. She moved on as I curtsied again, pledging loyalty.

Walking alongside her carriage, I took my place between her window and my achievements. Surely the crowd sensed our strong union.

Though my long dress marked me as a woman, my overcoat matched the male staff, and a cravat with a pin tucked into my fitted vest sent a clear message: I belonged among those I led.

Thoughts drifted to my father. Though his sons inherited precious possessions, he had reserved one for me, his daughter—his pocket watch. He foresaw my rise in status; this endowment would mark me as a woman of means. I wore it proudly, tucked in my vest pocket, attached by a gold chain. The Queen noticed.

Look the part you want to be, I thought, feeling the crowd's gaze.

Resuming my duties, I pulled out the watch and checked it before calling for an early lunch. The manager gestured uncertainty.

Her Highness surveyed the shipments. Each crate bore marks indicating its destination: India's crates held red circles like the locals' forehead dots; England's carried a 'T' with a longer horizontal; Portugal's bore a sideways 'S' shaped like a rooster.

Privately, the Queen praised my system. "I like this. It removes control from anyone beyond you. I often must usurp my possessions without the knowledge of predecessors. With this system, anyone can be dismissed and replaced without disruption. You have leverage."

Our partnership grew as we rearranged her assets—physical and financial—earning mutual admiration. Her praise rekindled memories of our immortal union, though I never told her how deeply I felt it.

Sundara's regal presence was captivating, yet the crown proved a cage, coloring a necessary but terrible lesson.

What the world imposed kept us from our greater path. The soul that loved beauty, believing her access of it was endless, spent a lifetime putting others first. She bore responsibility with grace, but it wore holes in her spirit, draining her energy until empty.

Our greatest gift became clear. Sundara turned inward, reclaiming her power, becoming peer to me—Aadyha—who had found freedom to rest.
The universe judges not. Her wish to spread beauty worldwide became a curse; her deepest comfort nearly lost itself in giving. Our bond was her sole comfort.

Tired and transformed, we embraced new boundaries, preparing for what lay ahead. Sundara wanted to be reborn into a path of self-care and personal limits.

I died then, a wife unknown to history but proud of the changes I helped bring —my husband's family business thriving, aiding many.
Returning to bliss, my life seemed simple beside a queen's. She had passed before me; I was surprised to find her waiting for my next cycle.
I recognized her instantly—when she first met me in the shipyard. Content, I knew she had realized our connection too now. Lost in space, but drawn to each other, I became her missing piece, her huckleberry.

How we circled, spinning reassured in the ether. No longer challenging fate, Sundara stayed close, her desire to complete our puzzle keeping us focused.

Reunited, she wondered what to do next. I feared more challenges, wanting safety in afterlife connection, avoiding life's pain.

Surprisingly, Sundara hoped for liberation and a free life. Our path was revealed in her vision. She wished to assume the roles of mother and daughter. I felt safe knowing the second born would be child to the first—our agreement filled with gratitude.

Long guiding others, she would now guide me in my next life. Without hesitation, she leapt forward; I delayed, observing.

"So be it!" exclaimed Sundara.

XXI: RECOLLECTION – FOREVER

Juniperus, a coniferous plant, bearer of protective seeds specially designed to safeguard inner gifts of life through unpredictable spans of time, awaiting the perfect moment to sprout from within.

Living independently, Sundara, this time, was a lady of the woods. Outside social norms, she gave birth to me as a single mother, naming me Juniper. We lived a fantastically lucky life, full of graceful meetings with others who shared our way of being.

Our spirits grew freely as we built an abundant homestead, a place overflowing with beauty and sustenance. The air there always smelled of cedar and sweet herbs. Bees hummed through lavender, and each sunrise seemed to pour gold over our roof. It was a sacred time of peace—until, without warning, the light began to fade.

Whispers of trouble rode on the wind. By the time I was twelve, nearby towns had turned to fear, hunting woodsmen and healers as if we were enemies. One by one, they were dragged away stabbed, hanged, drowned—for their misunderstood practices. I will always remember the day Sundara chose to give her life to protect the rest of us.

It was her land, her responsibility. She saw before anyone else what must be done. We left our gardens behind, urging our friends to scatter into hiding. But before we could slip away, armed men spotted us. Sundara turned toward me, her gaze steady, her love pouring across the space between us. Then she faced the inevitable.

That moment carved itself into my soul. I could feel her still looking at me, even as her body moved away. A thread stretched from her heart to mine, binding us in our shared dreamquest. So delicately fused together by impenetrable likeness, our spirits strengthened in the face of her sacrifice. If she had asked, none of us would have allowed her to trade herself. Yet she went as a queen would—unwavering, graceful, and fierce. I love you, I told her with my eyes. *This is not goodbye.*

The moment of her death was also the moment I felt her essence rush into me, a divine power that filled my small frame. I carried it, though it weighed heavily with grief.

In the days that followed, I longed for solitude. I was only twelve, but the crew looked to me for leadership. I resented life, yet I pressed forward, guiding them to rebuild in the deep woods.

Over time, the abandonment, the hate, the grief—they became a strange kind of fuel. I grew into my role, always feeling Sundara's presence watching from the ether. I wanted to live up to her, but there was one thing I craved more than her approval: absolute freedom.

When that life ended, I wished to return as a man, untethered. I was born into a Native American tribe, raised to live off the land, proud of my independence. I adorned myself with beads, charms, and stones—not for vanity, but to carry beauty with me, to keep the familiar energy of love near.

Seasons turned. The nomadic life taught me simplicity, yet grief found me again when colonization swept in like a dark tide. I learned that no lifetime was free from challenge, no gender immune from loss.

From her rest in bliss, Sundara reached for me in dreams. She showed me the truth—that our instinct to live close to the Great All would always expose us to the larger patterns moving through the world. Suffering belonged to the physical plane, and yet so did feeling, beauty, and love.

I began to wonder: should I ever return? Her answer was patient but certain. She showed me a vision of the coming century—a flood of knowledge, a return of ancient truths. A time ripe for awakening.

Braver than I, Sundara went first. I lingered in the ether, watching her choose the perfect souls to carry our dreams. She became a mother again, her children the seeds of our shared purpose. Her efforts left me amazed and rejuvenated by her powerful force to overcome.

Ingeniously, my timeless friend was meeting my hesitations with some very attractive options. Beaming with pride, I felt a deep closeness to the irresistible possibilities she laid before me.

Finally, following the twists and turns of our connection until ultimate understanding—reviewing all she had done to remain steady on the journey to reveal our deepest legacy—my courage was revived. I stepped forward, honoring my loyalty. And after five births preceding my own, I was born again as Sundara's daughter.

XXII: PRESENT TIME

As the cycles of time continue, so do the whispers of lives lived and lessons learned. You know me now as the adventurer, Aadya, but in the echoes of my soul, I am still the child of many worlds. I am Sundara's descendant, the youngest child of Cynthia Emerlye, and the thread that connects these vast legacies. These pages trace the road I have traveled, one that stretches back through eons of time and across many lifetimes, carving an avenue for the gifts of harmony passed down to me.

Our story spans the ages—spiritual truths woven through generations. These recollections from past lives manifest now, and in the spaces between, you'll see how they continue to shape me, how our ancient past guides the present moment. Together, my mother and I, with all our wisdom and love, have found a way to awaken through every life we've shared.

As I sit here now, in the present, I can feel the vibrations of the past still echoing around me. I remember those moments when I first began to understand the truth of who I am. The lessons passed down from time still resonate deep within me. My own spirit, like my mother's, helped to shape the person I've become, guiding me toward a deeper connection with the universe and with all those who came before.

Now, I will piece together what of my life has brought me to today; to write this book which continues to reveal our journey, together with Emerlye Arts.

***

Quieting myself into meditation, I feel the spirit of the Navajo shaman's daughter; the little girl from the red Moab desert. Her familiar sense brings back her spiritual melody; the subtle vibration rings in my memory. I often revisit the first time I smelled the fragrances from her grandmother's home. Though new to me in my earlier existence, even as a child, the incense seemed familiar.

When my mother brought our family to Utah, I remember how the native girl and I would watch and listen, quietly observing the feeling around us. Sometimes, we would fall into a trance, staring off into the distance, sensing that all the goodness in the universe emanated into the room.

Though I had just turned three years old—meaning this was long ago—I recall wondering why everyone wasn't always in a state of meditation, just as those reflections had taught me. Life seemed euphorically different there than anywhere else.

My many brothers and my sister teasing me is what I remember most from home at that time. I had contracted chickenpox from the shaman's grandchild.

In the '80s, parents intentionally exposed children early in hopes of protecting them from shingles later. There is still a mark on my right cheekbone from scratching one of the scabs; a permanent reminder of my friend. Sometimes, when I see the scar in the mirror, I feel that other girl was the closest I ever came to meeting someone so similarly raised.

Finally, my last feeling of our Native American friends was when my family was moving. I noticed my mother was upset, but I was too young to understand that we would never revisit that old woman and her granddaughter.

Before we left, I cannot forget the shaman turning to me after she embraced us both, clasping special necklaces around my neck. The wise grandmother's presence was enchanting. After sharing so much, we had developed a closeness.

Because of my time with my mother and that elder woman, I was forever fascinated by the idea that my soul could translate some frequency of understanding beyond basic comprehension.

I recall moving locations without fear, later defining worries about how different I might be based purely on others' reactions in the new place. Eventually, I found myself avoiding any public displays of spirituality. Growing through school years, I just wanted to fit in.

Though still evolving, I rebelled against fate, fighting myself with self-imposed pressure not to seek answers from deep within my soul.

Moving to Vermont, watching my mother and grandparents make the long haul from Utah, my siblings and I were all under sixteen. It's obvious now how colossal that undertaking was, leading our arrival during an epic snowstorm.

When we landed at our giant colonial rental in the bitter cold darkness, my siblings began to awaken, each voicing complaints about the cold weather. It was the middle of the night. Everyone was still groggy.

The snow was higher than I was when I hopped out of the van. My sudden disappearance alerted my mother until I climbed back in the car, laughing because I loved to get a rise out of my best friend.

The powder was so beautifully white and fluffy. The older kids asked why they didn't just drive back to Massachusetts instead? I always loved being with them all, relishing the chance to go unnoticed while watching the family dynamics.

Unable to manage around the snowpack, I patiently waited for someone to help me into the new colonial house. Finally, someone must have carried me.

The place was filled with old creaky wooden floors and outdated furnishings, but the most memorable to me as a child were the doorknobs—each with old latches and gaping keyholes. Every threshold had a hole to be opened by a skeleton key that could open every door in the house. In a spooky voice, my mother told me she held one in her deep, dark pocket.

I remember peering into each bedroom to see everyone exploring. It's barely memorable to me now, but we were there, as well as in another rental down the road, before landing on my mother's final choice in Pomfret.

***

XXIII: VERMONT CHILDHOOD

Seeking beauty creates a compass, pointing us to uplift the spirit.

When we moved into our family home in Vermont, I quickly learned it was the kind of place that held stories underground. We dug up rusted hand tools and green-glass bottles from the early 1900s, horseshoes buried like secret luck charms in the garden beds. Out back stood a weathered 1790s one-room schoolhouse, once inhabited by a blacksmith — perhaps the reason for the iron talismans scattered in the soil.

The house sat in an enchanted hollow, surrounded by rolling hills and a brook that whispered year-round. The stream fed two ponds — one uphill, one downhill — just a barefoot walk from the house for summer swimming or fishing. Apple trees bowed with fruit, rhubarb returned faithfully each spring, and everything seemed to hum with the rhythm of an older world.

Mom, restless in her new country life, decided we should become farmers. Two pigs were our first venture — and our first disaster. They escaped constantly. One early morning, Old Mr. Potter, our neighbor, knocked on the door with a grin: "The bacon's loose!" The next thing I knew, we were racing around the barn in pajamas, shouting and laughing while Mom tried to keep her patience.

A new future publication sprouted from our trials began to make its way into Mom's diaries. She called it, *Flatlanders* — about our family, transplanted into tough Vermont living without any experience.

We added sheep to the mix, staked in the front yard on long leashes — our naïve version of rotational grazing — which mostly made the neighbors shake their heads. Then Heather's "sister" rabbits arrived, one of whom promptly produced a surprise litter. Within two months, the babies had babies. We were drowning in rabbits. Most were released into the wild; only Skittles and Chocolate Milk remained.

I spent just as much time at my best friend Lindsey's farm up the road. The Christmas she was given a black pony named Rose, I became her eager helper. Together on their organic dairy farm we cared for cows, ponies, pigs, chickens, dogs, cats, guinea pigs, and even a ram. My bond with animals grew deeper, as did my sense of connection to the natural world. My mother even designed the pretty label for Lindsey's family's home-crafted cheese, a French, spicy cheese they named after the region of its recipe, Tarentaise — the work of art sealing our life-long friendship.

My mom didn't shy away from the raw parts of life either. One spring, she found a beaver dead by the roadside. Wearing winter gloves from the safety pack in her trunk, she carried it home and, with the calm precision of a science teacher, dissected it for us to see. I remember pressing my hand to my stomach, feeling the difference between a living body and one without a soul. It was my first intimate meeting with life's fragility.

It was also around that time I first saw the quiet magic others sometimes noticed in her. One humid morning, she and my brother Adam wandered the yard with copper rods in hand. I stayed quiet, watching the shimmer of heat over the grass, sensing something ancient in the air. They led me down to the basement, where a puddle spread into the dirt near the stone foundation. Mom explained how water was seeping in — and how they had been using dowsing rods to locate where to drive something into the ground that would guide it away.

That day, it worked. The dripping stopped.

I once asked her why no one else seemed to believe in dowsing. She told me of a pastor who'd said we would "go to hell" for trusting her spirit instead of God. That was why she chose to raise us without religion. "Do you think that's true?" she asked. "No," I answered.

Later that day, a blue heron glided alongside our car before landing in a stream. It locked eyes with me through the window — as if delivering a message. I didn't tell my mom. Some enchantments were best kept close until I could understand them, I felt.

Without realizing it, I had already stepped onto the path she walked — a path of symbols, spirit, and quiet instruction — and once that door opens, it never really closes.

***

XXIV: COLORED INTO CARPE DIEM

Allow the universe to flow through openings from change, attracting feelings of spiritual gain into your life as you advance the infinite timeline of your soul's art.

I can still remember being too young to read when someone told me that if you tried, you could control your dreams. They called it lucid dreaming.

My parents had already taught me that my waking mind was a muscle I could train. This felt like my first true test.

When I tried, I succeeded. The next time I found myself in a nightmare, I reshaped it. Spiders and snakes dissolved into butterflies and bunnies. Entire scenes transformed to me on horseback, galloping through tall grass. It was intoxicating, this idea that even in sleep I could choose beauty over fear.

But one night, the rules shifted.

I awoke to see a small cloud-like ring of animals circling under a tent in my bedroom. They glowed faintly, spinning in a slow, silent loop. It should have been whimsical, but in the dark, it was ghostly. I know now it was a carousel. At the time, it was simply impossible because I was awake. My control failed me.

I ran to my mother's room. For a long time after, I avoided opening my eyes at night. My magic only worked behind my eyelids.

My mother, the dreamwalker in my life, never dismissed the experience. She spoke of dreams as a realm where answers live, where our souls go to work, where we are both the architects and the inhabitants. Even when I was nervous in the dark, she made me feel that the dreamworld was an inheritance worth protecting.

That same year, two events changed everything.

The first was the stock market crash. By Christmas, my mother was deep in the lawsuit of her life against Morgan Stanley, fighting for the divorce settlement she'd entrusted to them. She had believed her broker would act with the caution a single mother of six needed. Instead, everything was placed in short-term, high-risk investments.

I remember her standing in the living room, holding back tears, reading out a list of stocks and asking which ones we thought she should keep or sell. We had no idea, and neither did she. My father, who'd sent her to that broker without knowing him very well, had already burned through his own side of the money on failing startups.

At one point, I slipped upstairs to where an old Macintosh sat in a closet. Apple stock was on her list. I didn't speak up, but I stared at the bitten logo, wishing I could keep what I felt as a bright thing in our life.

When the court ruled against her, we were left with less than a hundred thousand dollars of the original multiple millions. The house was safe, but the rest unraveled. My mother canceled plans for a horse stall she'd promised me. That Christmas, she announced a new rule for the expensive holiday: four gifts each. A winter coat wasn't among them. I remember my youthful shame crossing my face when asking if Santa could bring one instead, not understanding yet that Santa's budget came from the same place as hers but realizing it when she began to cry again.

The second event was quieter but just as profound.

My mother began focusing on selling her artwork for income instead of treating it as a pastime. Without realizing it, I became her apprentice. I watched her sketch for days, erase, refine, and finally trace perfect lines in ink before layering on color.

One day, she asked me to model. I was eager to be part of her process, to have her focus on me the way she did on her drawings. Draped in a sheet to bare my shoulders, I sat on her bed, staring into the large gilded mirror at its foot. Sitting still felt endless. To calm myself, I went inward just as I did in my dreams, focusing on the discomfort without resisting it. That moment became the seed of a lifelong coping strategy.

When she revealed the finished piece, I was stunned. She had drawn me as the Grim Reaper, dark cloak, scythe in hand, an owl perched on its blade. She explained that Death is not an enemy but a guide, escorting souls when their time comes. I didn't understand it was meant to be me. The owl made sense; wisdom I could relate to. But the hummingbirds, symbols of spiritual transformation, felt too distant from my childhood self. The cloak and scythe frightened me, especially when she reminded me that my astrological chart linked me to the underworld.

She titled it *Carpe Diem*. To me, that meant lifting my arms to the sky and squeezing as much fun as possible into a single day. The idea of seizing life because death is inevitable was far beyond my reach.

Another portrait drawn from that same sitting was easier to love. In it, a girl with wavy red hair, part me, part my mother, part my sister, wore a golden crown carved with the hours of time. The sun and moon spun around her head. My mother called it *Universe Girl*. I understood that one instantly.

Over the years, I saw how her art and our lives seemed to move in tandem, revealing meanings she could never have planned.

When I look back now, I see the quiet power in those moments, lucid dreams, market crashes, bare-shouldered portraits. Modeling for Emerlye Arts wasn't just about posing. It was a rehearsal for becoming the thing itself: the bridge between life and death, the traveler of dreams, the one who learns slowly, over years, to seize the day.

***

XXV: Grasping the Awakening

I was full of youthful arrogance, overly confident in my abilities, and started getting into trouble. Life seemed too easy, and following a straight, dedicated path felt restrictive, as though it was holding me back from a special life meant to be lived differently. Forgetting the lesson from my time in Egypt, I thought to myself, "What if I could do better than what the universe would provide?" I was so naive—impatient, full of myself, and underutilized, convinced that there was more to explore beyond the narrow confines of my small world.

Like many mischievous teens, I would sneak out of my mother's home in Pomfret, climbing into the rusted old Toyota Corolla passed down through my siblings. Breaking the rules made life more thrilling, especially when I was still blissfully ignorant of real danger. Like every teen, I just wanted to be with my friends.

The Corolla had seen many owners—my wild, metal-music-blasting sister Heather, my gentle brother Joshua who forgot to put oil in it and so had it taken away early, then, finally, Benjamin, my ADHD brother. Each time, the car was handed down, with the hope that we would all learn responsibility from it.

Ben was the most comedic and unusual of us. Although angelic and Buddha-like in his demeanor, his actions were often outlandish. I'll never forget the day we were in a Woodstock grocery store parking lot, watching Ben pull up in the manual car, not even bothering to turn it off. It rolled forward in neutral, and I realized too late he'd steered the car into a shopping cart, which shot forward with a loud bang! People gawked as the car continued rolling unattended, and Ben just walked away laughing.

I quickly realized it was my job to take control. I jumped in, took the wheel, and brought the car back to its rightful place, the crazy chaos somehow enhanced the exciting fun of getting my first car.

There were other moments taken in from that new ride in my life too, late at night, when I'd sneak out and notice a white bird following me in Ol' Rusty as we wound through curving roads. I would see it out of the corner of my eye—its feathers glowing faintly in the darkness. It was always there. One cold night, I mentioned it to my mom.

"You know," she said casually, "Owls are watchdogs for danger. They're all-seeing, all-knowing."

That owl became my silent warning. I was ignoring the dangers of my actions, and soon enough, I would learn that ignoring the signs only led to greater consequences.

It was around that time, during the early millennium, that a new shift began to happen. People started talking about a coming awakening, a time when spirituality would no longer be hidden but celebrated. The internet was bringing forth this surge of awareness, and the world was beginning to accept individuality and spiritual expression once again.

However, this change seemed to conflict with my mother's fear of judgment. Though she embraced my beliefs, she hesitated to share them publicly. She was still cautious about being too open with her gifts, and I felt that frustration deep inside. She, too, had a gift for guiding people, but she wasn't ready to embrace the larger world in the way I had. I wanted to promote her services, to show people what she could offer, but her hesitation held me back.

Despite this, I knew that I had a destiny—our destinies were connected, and I felt a deep knowing that we were meant for something greater, something that could unite the world in ways we hadn't yet understood.

I decided to push forward, to take the first step toward what I believed was inevitable—taking the chance to see how far I could carry this path of discovery.

After a tumultuous time in Vermont, a part of me still sought something more. I was confused by my situation—unsure of where I wanted to go, but craving more than the small world I knew. I sold my car and took a big step. I decided on taking my senior year abroad. The flight was over 21 hours, and when I left Pomfret Springs, I left with a sense of finality, but also with a deep awareness of what I loved most and what I was meant to treasure.

During my time in New Zealand, I came to understand that trying to control fate with logic was misguided. Upon returning, my bond with my mother grew stronger than ever. She was my guide, my teacher, and I sought her wisdom like never before.

I needed her more than I realized. Her words brought me comfort, her lessons gave me clarity. We had a quiet car ride one day where I confessed my struggles, saying, "Now that I'm back, some kids seem to have everything figured out. I don't know what to look forward to. The way they're all planned out frustrates me." She responded simply, "No one can make you feel anything. You are the master of yourself. Your much too young to need worry about time. Just focus yourself on happiness and try new things until that practice brings joy into your work." Her words lifted me, bringing relief to my confused, restless heart.

***

XXVI: ADVENTURE

After my time in New Zealand, I found myself drawn back to a life that felt more aligned with my true path. I worked at Keadron Valley Stables in South Woodstock, immersing myself in my passion for horses and the quiet, purposeful beauty that came with caring for them. The simplicity of stable life, the connection to the earth, resonated deeply within me.

My mom's artistic journey flourished while I was away, and I realized that I, too, was awakening. I had grown, learning lessons in patience, understanding, and the natural unfolding of life. College offered a taste of structure after that—I tried Equine Business Management, then Environmental Studies at the University of Vermont—but freedom was my true teacher, and the wild, living world became my classroom.

After collage I returned home again. Though financially independent, my mom worried, hoping I would find stability. Leaving her felt like loosening the last tether to childhood, yet she encouraged me to spread my wings.

Even as I charted my own path, the roots of my spirit ran deep in Vermont. I remembered being the youngest, sent alone down the road to join a preschool class called *The Rainbow Room*, nestled at the foot of Mt. Tom, a great winter sledding hill. In warmer months, we wandered behind the school, exploring the woods, learning the names of plants. Not unlike my days at home, I was unknowingly training as a little environmentalist, learning to nurture life in all its forms as a youngster, before Kindergarten.

That early chapter of Vermont life became a cornerstone of my dreamquest, the first lesson in how to witness life and its mysteries, fully present, fully myself.

Trusting my inner guidance, I moved west to Portland, Oregon, a city I intuitively knew would be the right place for me. There, I was reunited with Lindsey. After drifting apart for several years, discovering she lived in Portland felt like the touch of serendipity I needed to realign my journey.

She helped me move into a grim townhouse—very different from Pomfret's fairy-tale farm—with a frightening sign at the entrance: a darkly painted goat wearing a top hat and sporting a stern expression. That small, odd dwelling sparked my courage, and I soon moved into a modest apartment downtown.

Finding work in a new city proved challenging; business owners expressed their fear of hiring someone who seemed transient, and opportunities were scarce. I asked Lindsey for guidance, and she provided a reference that opened the door to my next job.

I started working at a local pizza place, delivering their pies around the town, learning the lay of the land while driving the provided hybrid car. It was decorated with a big, red, smooching kiss to represent their name, Hot Lips Pizza. I laughed often again and felt more at home than ever.

My path seemed unpredictable, but it was following its own course—a course of growth, friendship, and quiet triumph. I was starting to understand that the invisible thread of fate had been guiding me all along.

***

XXVII: SPIRITUAL FARMER

After about one year, I moved from Oregon to California to pursue a more direct career aligned with my nature loving background. The purpose was to advance my newest entrepreneurial venture. Then, after one very successful season working to industrially farm with a partner, the following year I managed two leased business properties on my own.

My mom decided she would visit for my birthday that second year. She was excited to see my efforts to farm multiple properties with several people working as my helping aids. We were both proud that my love for the environment and my wishes for financial stability had combined toward a career in growing agricultural crops.

I was living where I could earn my piece of the current Green Rush. Returning to my destined role to lead a large existence, I had invited several girlfriends to also arrive when Sundara did. I had one wish: that they all visit dressed as Disney princesses. I hoped we could see how lovely life could become when aligned with our greatest path of free-spirited energy.

Ariel flew in from Vermont. Cinderella traveled from Florida. Princess Jasmine made a scenic trip across the country. Pocahontas worked on the farm. Elsa helped prepare with us. Belle and Anastasia were our friends from down the road, and I dressed as Tiger Lily.

On the day of celebration, we all had a great amount of fun with my Mumsy, who came as our precious Fairy Godmother. Her magical wand, created from one of the farm's budding branches, added enchantment to our day. After much research about the new industry I'd chosen for myself, she proved our bond was unbreakable once again, joining fully in the spirit of my venture. She even asked me to take her photo in front of the farm's largest plant, one that grew monstrously tall like a tree.

Aside from those organized operations, I had rented a wonderful apartment. I was in a prime location in a town called Arcata. It had lots of natural light, was pet-friendly, and offered a good price, so I kept it for a long time. The best part was the ocean view from my front window, looking down at a dozen red-and-white Hereford cows grazing by the waterfront. I used to joke after a rainstorm that my cows looked pretty good—"now they're all washed off!"

One morning, I had awakened from a nap in a nearby field when part of my greater dreamquest revisited with important lessons. I looked up to see the most beautiful flurry of dragonflies soaring above me in a circling dance, filling the span of a half-acre.

I began to feel it was important that I was there right at the moment, continuing to allow myself to follow key interpretations of my lifelong journey. Momentum had continued building for that sort of communication reaching my spirit from the ether. Examples of what I was discovering were unfolding in front of me because I was awakened now, finally noticing with ease the subtle hints I was being called to translate.

Once I revisited publications about their meaning, the dragonflies revealed my newest lesson. What I discovered about their spiritual symbolism helped me comprehend yet another truth to consider. The creatures, I understood, are only in flight for a very short time compared to how long they exist as crawling insects. Incredibly, their two body phases within one lifetime are quite different.

First, they begin eating and resting, wingless on the ground, until finally transforming into an insect resembling a dragon's tail with wings. Furthermore, between their two different shapes, they are suspended inside a chrysalis, just as butterflies are, when the impossible happens. Encapsulated within its own mumification, the dragonfly completely melts down into liquid, returning to resemble an entirely new body afterward.

To become engulfed within a self-destructive coffin only to rise as a completely different being with wings was fascinating and extraordinary. The amount of information they must process after their transformation may compare to spiritual awakening, I pondered. Once fully matured, they can maneuver in unlimited directions, hovering in the air with even greater ability than a helicopter.

Observing the show of winged fairy-like ballerinas in the field above, I was sure they were paying close attention to me. They made a remarkable sight as they flew back and forth. I knew that to become part of this lesson, I would have to trust the process of metamorphosis—but how?

Causing oneself discomfort to grow exponentially seemed terrifying. The symbolism from the universe was telling me to gather what I had, build a chrysalis, and melt down, allowing new transformation. But I wasn't heeding that advice. Success was blinding. The important dreamwalk message was attempting to guide me through what was to come, which would halt everything and challenge my newly earned savings.

Tempted only by curiosity, I dangerously wondered what would happen if I stayed the course as I was. Soon afterward, I was still farming when I stumbled upon an astrology reading at a benefit for a local eatery. Though my mother had shared the star alignment interpretations gathered for me as a child, I wanted a new reading.

The woman astrologer told me many aspects I had not already heard. I remembered the negativity from the first reading; now this current translation was quite to the contrary. The "underworld" was not bad at all, she informed me. My previous interpretations of it were replaced—it was simply the afterlife.

Rather than remaining intimidated by my chart, I now felt realigned to my destiny again. I was relieved. Though I still didn't understand it clearly, I recalled my mother's spiritual art at that moment, specifically the drawing where my younger self vowed to seize the day.

I was glad to be earning enough money to follow my desires because the ability to disregard distractions was reinforced. However, I still had trouble remaining loyal to my dreamwalking hints when they conflicted with my fear of risking financial security above all else.

In the end, nothing could alter my strong belief that everything would reveal itself in due time, whether or not I listened or carried out the callings. Still ignorant of exactly why, but as if strengthened by our quest together during her visit, once returned home, I heard my mother was gravely ill and in the hospital.

Losing Sundara was incomprehensible. That was it—the reason I should have had everything stored up and saved, ready to melt down emotionally, but had not listened.

Remembering before her pain began, before there were any signs of her illness, I could feel deeply that things were not fine for many years. But without the intensity of impending separation, I had not realized everything we had before now.

I always shared my worries with her prior to that devastating phone call. She would say she felt it too, and we would release our worries once more to continue blissfully ignorant, ignoring our gifts out of fear.

Rushed to return to Vermont with so much hope, I believed my mother could be treated. After all, she was only sixty-six!

Upon my arrival, I resolved not to leave her side until she was cured. Unfortunately, back in Northern California, I had several people managing my leased properties when I frantically departed, and I had not hired according to my absence. As my lesson, I lost half of my savings in one season when I wasn't present. I should have listened to the dragonflies. Instead, I learned the hard way to always heed spiritual communication aligned enough within my life to make its monumental transitions through many layers of existence to bring me powerful understanding.

***

Soon after, to make matters worse, my mom's mother, Nana, was also terminal. Edith Adelaide gave the sad news herself by voice. It was January of the same year when Nana told us she would transcend very soon. She requested everyone come say goodbye by the time my mother was hospitalized in the summer.

The news seemed bizarre because Nana sounded well over the phone. How could anyone predict their death so surely? She was trying to maintain a good mood about her life ending, saying she desired the adventure of moving on. Her husband did not like the thought of what she offered. I can never forget the way Grampa Morry took pleasure in feeding her, or how she would eat it all with a smile. To humor him, she sought a diagnosis.

During my many visits, Nana Edith's teeth were beginning to crack and fall out. She bravely laughed about her body's decline: "Back to dust," she said, laughingly, as if she'd better get out of it first!

I pictured her with a rare smile as she waited to look upon the Angel of Death. To everyone, she kept repeating, "Remember you are loved." Those same words now read on her gravestone in the oceanside cemetery in Rhode Island, where she was placed early that December.

XXVIII: SANTA CRUZ

Ultimately, life had slowed down in Pomfret while I cared for my patient. Remaining close, I had no other desire than to be with her. Earlier, she had often phoned my grandmother—both distantly aware, yet hopeful they were not crossing into the afterlife around the same time. Now, returning with my whole family from Nana's burial service, I lay quietly on Mumsy's special couch by the grand fireplace. I regretted the precious moments I had spent away from her. It was comforting to think that her own mother may have transcended the pain before facing her daughter's end.

Suddenly, while resting my mind on the sofa, a notion came: *"Santa Cruz."* The location shocked me, originating from a dreamwalk I had begun but not completed the previous year. That spring, before knowing my mother's illness would progress further, I had followed the dragonflies' message and driven south from Arcata on Highway 101, searching for the best place to live next.

I wanted to open the first physical Emerlye Arts store, realizing my best life would involve using my business skills to help my mother's gifts reach the world. I considered opening the space on my own, inviting my mom to visit frequently once it was up and running.

I researched the prettiest coastal towns in California, seeking a location that would serve as a meaningful getaway. Though we agreed that Vermont would always be our home, it was too underpopulated, forcing my mom to sell most of her art online—a system that could be managed anywhere, I thought.

I first considered La Jolla, then drove to Santa Monica, Malibu, Ventura, Santa Barbara, Carmel-by-the-Sea, Santa Cruz, Los Gatos, and San Francisco, leaving my car for as long as needed at each stop to feel the vibe of the small shops and galleries. Ten days of searching passed. Some towns swept me away more quickly than others, yet in the end, it was clear where we belonged. Santa Barbara seemed perfect for both of us—art scene, traffic, landscape, and lifestyle—but Santa Cruz called to me personally in a way I couldn't yet understand.

It was winter, after my mother attended her own mother's funeral, and I worried the icy Vermont weather would put her at risk. Gathering my research, I rented an apartment in Santa Cruz for us. The rent was more than triple what I had ever paid monthly, but I trusted it would be worth it.

Emerlye's first response was to resist Santa Cruz, then she changed her mind. I did not push her to leave Vermont. Yet, as I pointed out, all my siblings were indisposed with children and partnerships—where I was not.

Before committing, I called the landlord to explain why we were staying from January to May. His voice was so familiar that I lost myself in wonder. Transfixed, I asked him to repeat himself. The oddness of the phone call stayed with me.

Upon moving in, I hired two female helpers to assist with whatever was needed. Spoiling my mom with a jacuzzi and a small staff felt wonderful. Although expensive, the trade was worth it. I was filled with gratitude that she was safe and that we could be by the ocean. The smell of the sea reminded her of Rhode Island. We made new friends among the neighbors and lived comfortably.

Not long after moving in, while I was away on a short work trip, my mother met the landlord in person. His name was Tushar Atre, a green-eyed Indian man raised in New York City who owned a successful tech company. Charismatic and kind, he offered his assistance in any way he could. When I heard he had taken my mom to a place known as *The Medicine Buddha*, a serene wooded landscape with meditative trails, I was overjoyed.

My doting mother had so many good things to say about Tushar. She was obviously concerned for my future, hoping to see me in a safe, long-term relationship. I told her not to be silly by persuading our connection but that, somehow, I recognized his voice the first time I heard it. It felt as though we had already met.

Curiously, a few weeks later, alone in our rental, a strange occurrence unfolded. Just as I walked in from outside, the television turned on by itself. A live scene from a traditional Indian wedding played. A young girl knelt while other women tattooed her hands and feet with henna. The room filled with Bollywood music.

Even more astonishingly, the television changed on its own again, now playing my mother's favorite video on YouTube: Sam Bailey from the UK singing *"New York"* by Frank Sinatra. I squealed. Hearing me, my mom rolled her walker over, and together we stared in wonder.

She was on painkillers, making spiritual guidance impossible at the time, yet she smiled. Rationally, I thought Tushar must be fooling with us, but how could he have known Cynthia loved Sam Bailey? Holding onto her walker, we joined in the chorus: *"It's up to you, New York, New Yoooorrrk!"*

Afterward, I invited Tushar to witness what had happened. He entered and sat cross-legged on the floor, watching rather than participating. We played the song again, along with several others, laughing and enjoying the moment. Eventually, he explained that he wasn't very "techie" himself, merely managing computer professionals, and denied any role in the strange events.

XXIX: RETURN HOME

A year of blissful solitude with my mom led to a moment of loving closure back in Vermont. It was deep summer. Neither of us had ever flown first class before. There's a special kind of peace when you can spend last moments together without worrying about money.

Onboard, nestled in wide seats, I introduced Mumsy to noise-canceling headphones. We giggled over fluffy socks and reclined fully, lying flat as if in beds. To some, it might've seemed silly, but to us, it was pure delight—more spoiled than ever.

Still, it was impossible to ignore the pain in her hip. For years, before we knew cancer was present, she had endured a dull ache. Now, it was excruciating.

We reclined quietly, watching movies, and I tried to hold my emotions in check.

My mind drifted to Santa Cruz—to earlier that morning when we made our last descent down the stairs of Tushar's retreat and into a waiting taxi. She turned, sat carefully on her reversed walker, and pulled me into her lap for what felt like the final time.

I resisted at first, laughing through tears. "Mom! I'm too big for this." But eventually, I gave in, careful not to lean into her frail frame, pretending to sit. I wept silently behind her, where she couldn't see.

She smiled, full of pride and comfort. Her strength, even then, felt beyond tears. The warmth we shared felt eternal—more than just for me. Somehow, I knew it would last forever, beyond either of our lives, though I couldn't explain how.

Overwhelmed by love for all she was leaving behind—her art, fashion, wisdom—I teared up again as she ran her fingers gently through my hair.

"You are my special angel," she whispered, "you'll always be my baby."

I kept my eyes lowered, trying to hide my breaking heart. I saw how noble her work was, right there before me. Laughing off my deeper feelings, I pleaded with her not to worry about me.

Then, embodying the strength of a pain-free soul, she reached for my chin and looked straight into me. In that moment, she was Sundara, and I was Aadyha. We were meant for something greater, though it felt suddenly unfinished.

I couldn't hold her gaze. I knew if a single tear slipped, it would unleash a flood I couldn't stop. She'd see it. It would hurt her.

I needed to stay strong, for her. I saw the pain it caused her to witness my grief. We both knew I was losing her physical body soon. Worse, she knew it too.

There had always been something comforting about leaving the body—like the peace after deep meditation, a dreamy rest. But this time, I knew it was different. Once she crossed into bliss, she wouldn't come back.

Her crossing felt like a recurring dream—one in which we both knew we were destined to lose each other. Though painful, it still somehow felt worth it.

As I rose from her lap, I was struck by how brutal life can be. I wondered why we choose to come here again; why we return to a world where love is destined to break our hearts.

In that moment, I remembered her saying, with quiet sorrow, "I'm sorry I let you get so used to me always being with you. Maybe I shouldn't have."

Of course, I disagreed. How could I not?

Once we arrived in Vermont, she smiled, confessing it had been the best choice to return home. She was so happy we hadn't chosen a hospital.

The renowned local artist lit a candle for all to see. She called everyone in to bid farewell with love. Visitors came from everywhere, returning the special feeling they harbored for her work. Admiring her talents was the best way to support Cynthia Emerlye. Talking about her prolific art collection was like attending a wonderful show where she was the producer.

Loved ones from her celebrated art therapy work drove down from a halfway house called Second Springs Farm to honor her.

Already decided, with her legacy around us, knowing I could do anything with my life, I finally shared my exuberant discovery with her: we were linked beyond all lifetimes. She enjoyed the reciprocity of good feelings as I revealed my plans to establish her art through business and writing this story.

Though supportive in her quest to uplift, Mumsy, physically present yet clouded by pharmaceuticals, quietly urged me to focus on my career with plants. Afraid I would retire in squalor following her path as a starving artist, she trusted what I was already succeeding at.

I knew Emerlye undervalued her legacy simply because it was unfinished. Many self-published works sold alongside published ones, and her most popular sales came from a meditation coloring journal called *A Tangle of Flowers*. The workbook revealed Mom's fairytale soul, with the information based on poetry from true life entwined with fantastical floral imagery.

At the time, I didn't realize how vital her legacy would be to my healing as I revisited all she'd created. I spread everything saved on an antique rug in front of the fireplace, jotting notes and planning.

It brought back a memory for me on top of this rug she had bought on the way back from Utah. I had sat one day making a collage for her. During the moments after we spoke about the collage, she had told me that, when she bought that rug she was in the middle of a bizarre in Pennsylvania. The crowded place where all sorts of things were being sold was taken to silence when a man dropped to his knees in front of my mother and said to her, "It is you! I know it is. It is you."

She asked the man to please get up. Dressed in nice clothes, he was acting as if he was not with his own mind. She told me, this was not the first time that anyone in the world had come to her saying that she had special aura or something about her was very familiar to them. It was as if he knew her from a time long ago, she said, and he was sure that she had some gift, some special way of giving from herself to the world.

Now, as I peer down again at the journal, I realize its teaching are about how to focus on what uplifts. She had, in fact, given gifts to the world, but now they would be frozen in time unless someone could carry them forth again. It led me to decide to bring her work and her methods further into the world.

Setting aside the journal as my clear favorite, I couldn't resist her ocean of artwork. The collection was extensive—hundreds of drawings in different sets. The pile was surprisingly high until I organized everything into storage.

I thought of how my mom explained the origin of each piece. I brought her back to life whenever I spoke of them. What brought me to life was seeing her light up when others loved her work. Each creation revealed the universe's beauty.

Supporting her final time, I paid a pianist to transcribe notes from an old recording my brothers saved—her song composed in youth, played at her wedding. Alongside her logo, the modern classic we named, *Emerlye,* rang loudly in her room those fall afternoons.

For Sundara, many gathered in her last weeks—family, friends, and fans—to share wisdom and follow her guidance. Divine in those moments, it was clear Beauty was trailblazing her crossing.

Though confused, those around her watched as she received spiritual guidance and love from her mother. Then the incredible happened: she cleared the room and closed her eyes for days.

As she weakened, her presence felt lighter, yet I saw her strength. After four years of pain, astonishingly, without medicine, she achieved peaceful existence.

Rarely speaking, she verbalized only what was essential. Once, when I asked about a potential visitor, her glassy eyes shone white with loss of all their bright color responded faintly, "No more flowers... three days."

Gracefully closing her eyes under dark brows, she repeated, "Three days."

Preserving her energy, I knew she had no strength or purpose left for more.

***

XXX: LAND OF THE KNOWING

Over the past final months, I watched as my mother journaled her inner world. Her expressions took shape as intricate carvings etched into clayboard—sacred engravings. One such carving depicted a flower losing its petals, like strands of hair, each one a quiet surrender. These works felt like ancient hieroglyphs—intimate and eternal, entries into her life's story.

Then, it became clear: all of her images wove together, unified in meaning, carrying not only her personal journey but the collective weight of many. Her final experience was part of something much larger, a connection to something timeless.

In a rush, I gathered what I could, setting up her art in rows—each piece a chapter of her cancer journey. As I stood there, the air seemed to shift. My siblings, who had been caring for her alongside me, sought brief respite elsewhere. Another blessing arrived: two full days alone with her, wrapped in silence and peace.

I spent that time meditating beside her. Not hungry or thirsty, I knew the end was near. As I sat, questioning her fate, I longed to feel closer to my own. She was emerging from her final chrysalis. I feared how swiftly she might vanish.

My body grew still alongside hers. From deep within, colors and visions opened in my mind—born from hours of reflection. My dear mother, weak yet delighted, cast small joys in those final hours. Each morning, she seemed calm, sensing the world around her. Even with her head tilted softly, I was amazed at how she could feel my gaze.

Time and again, when I silently looked at her, she responded—a slight smile, squinting eyes even when closed. It was as if she were listening to something beautiful, dreaming peacefully, still connected to me.

By then, she weighed almost nothing, like a child. I lifted her gently to adjust the bed. On the second morning alone, I carried her to her wheelchair, guiding the electric seat. We rolled into the sun, where she rested in the warmth. Just us, holding space in the final golden hours.

Tushar called. It was comforting to know someone who truly loved me would be there after her passing. Filled with desperation, I awoke to a final morning. As I descended the stairs, I was grateful to find Mumsy still breathing softly.

While quietly checking on her, a dream flashed in my mind from two nights before. In it, she was healthy, cleaning out the house. Like the Incredible Hulk, she powerfully threw things from windows into the street—a wild, disorganized yard sale. Her attitude was determined and pleased.

I remembered how she had carefully kept her one living-room couch pristine—pastel and lightest in the house, contrasting with darker tones elsewhere to hide children's messes. It was her treasure, protected for decades. Yet in the dream, she tossed it casually out a side window, letting it fall to the curb without a second thought.

I wasn't upset by her letting go of things—they were just things. But seeing her discard that couch so freely cut deep. It hurt, witnessing her release something so cherished.

More striking: it was the first dream I had of her truly alive. Vivid, lucid—more real than her body beside me.

The feeling terrified me. How could I feel her more fully in a dream than in waking life? Why would she throw away something so symbolic of care and consistency?

To me, that was a clear sign: she was done here. She had let go. She was ready to move on.

But I wasn't ready for her to leave me.

Clinging to hope, I told myself I was now the couch's keeper—its new owner, its protector. Returning to her side, I whispered the dream to her as she lay calm. Holding back tears, I told her what I believed: if she could choose her ending, maybe she had the power to stay longer.

To my amazement, she raised her eyebrows in quiet acknowledgment. Her expression was full of dignity and grace. It was as if she agreed with my interpretation, affirming her strength to remain—not through resistance—but as a gift, present with me still, free from pain.

I wanted her to know how proud I was to be her daughter. Relishing her presence, my thoughts fell on her last gestures.

First, she gave me her flower ring. The beauty of it fitting my finger perfectly after a lifetime of seeing it on her petite hand overwhelmed me.

When she took it off, I insisted she return it, but she slipped it onto me, telling me never to remove it unless it went into a bank box.

Next, she asked her messy country girl to please wear gloves.

I promised. My mom was a woman of gentility—living with decorum and etiquette. Emerlye wanted me to follow her example. Well-read and rich in quality, she lived a life beyond money.

After watching the ring slip on my hand, explaining how her wilder child should protect it, she pleaded, "And please speak as I taught you—no improper English... and the swearing..."

I promised everything before going outside to lie in the yard where no one could see me.

It was warmer than a typical October. Lying on thick grass, I pointed my toes to the sky, peering through tree branches at white fluffy clouds. The realization washed over me that I must learn to cope with loss. My mom would say, "Such is life."

Embracing death's visit, I admired how she documented her truth in monthly carvings. Premiering her visions, they held wisdom deeper than I'd known.

One carving showed her spiritual self—Sundara—smiling, long wild curls of Kali flowing weightlessly. She'd designed it before crossing over, drifting where the egret flies, hand grasping six flowers she would take in a bouquet with her.

Laying in her nest in Pomfret, I imagined her rising to comfort me while I struggled. I rested within my choice ahead. My fate would bring the power to lift into new inner growth—or fall, sinking with reluctance to let Mumsy fly away.

**

XXXI: TRANSCENDENCE

The language of ether is like a dream, how it is revealed does not make sense until a message emerges through awakening to find what will be.

My mother's kite had risen all the way to the last bit of its ties. Within the final critical days, there was a feeling all around her I couldn't explain. The essence of her slow transcendence of soul was most profound. It taught me to recognize how it feels in the subtle vibrations of the room when a spiritual being begins to separate from its body. That profound blessing, incredibly, proved my mother's premonition as an art medium for me was true: every ending must be a renewal; carpe diem, or else.

Understanding came now as the grim. My place is neither good nor evil, rather neutral, symbolizing the inevitability of death as a crucial part of living. Many important dreams prevailed, the show of each creating a pattern of revelation toward my ability to translate spiritual messages. I felt divinely persuaded to return upon the timeless continuation when I noticed something had already begun to come through me.

Another dream started with my mother's twinkling ring in it. It was broken. I held the pieces in my hand. To my horror, the center stone had fallen out. It was gone! The charming flower of ten white diamonds was missing some of the gleaming petals around its light purple amethyst.

Peering down, I came to see two loose diamonds remained in my other hand. The rest of the gems seemed intact on the gold band but the amethyst had disappeared.

I was worried about losing any more of the precious stones as I began searching for a jeweler in the dream who could repair the broken pieces. The only one I came across was not a skilled artisan. I had to wait for the right person who could do the repair.

Though I kept the pieces safely closed in my hand I was frantic. Just as I arose from it all, panicking and wishing my mother could help me, in the end of the dream I awoke to her saying, kindly, *"It was always meant to be an opal."*

The stress caused me to rise up, trembling with difficulty of the situation until it led me to a different vision. I saw myself a very young girl now, desiring to learn about my mother's gifts long ago. Feeling brought along a dreamwalk, I continued to recall more in tune, bringing a further message.

In the new memory I alone would resonate with, my mom had laid me upon a floral coverlet draped on her bed. Calmly closing my eyes and then hers, she wanted to practice Reiki, a way to visualize the essence of my spiritual energy, she said.

I was told she expected my aura to appear like a typical element—fire, water, air. Instead, what she described was endless, radiant colors reflecting from millions of tiny shapes, like a window to a separate galaxy. From what I remember, the essence of what she saw was all colors, very much indicative of an opal! A type of stone where each piece is completely unique, shining with reflections from everything around it.

Centered again in knowing I had learned from her how to perfect translation of my dreams and the inklings of spirit, I returned myself downstairs for this last morning.

The first thing Beauty did after parting from her body was come in spirit to my side, while I sat in another room. I was watching a pleasing scene from *The Lord of the Rings* in our movie den, overlooking the water rushing down the stream outside, when the words of love appeared. She seemed right next to me when, without her body, whispered words resounding with as much pride as pity came saying, *"Oh, my darling girl..."*

The message caused me to sit up. Though my heart was denying my intuition, hoping it would be wrong, I could never have ignored it. It finally hit me. I realized the important connection spirit has with everything because it was my last ultimate chance to remain connected in this precious moment.

Turning in the direction I heard her voice, she wasn't there. I responded, desperately knowing the truth, "Mom, no…" before, quietly, I dragged myself to the living room, where she remained peacefully laying, a sweetness brightening her face.

Looking around with lost hope I saw my brother nearby on the special pastel couch. He was sleeping. I guessed he had joined us in the night, just in time to dream next to her soft breathing, soothing him one last time.

Dropping into prayer, I silently wept. Begging for it not to be true, savoring my final moments alone with her. Kneeling by her bed, holding her warm, soft, still hand, I allowed my sobs to grow. Louder and louder, the sounds exited my breath with such tremendous grief I knew my brother would understand when he awoke.

Finally alert, he, too, found himself crippled by our mother's silent bedside. Soft chirping outside could be heard beyond the two nearby corner windows. Ethereal, white morning light shined in. Joshua and I laid across our mom embracing one another, holding very still before we phoned our other siblings.

Except, before any of them could arrive, a surprise would show up. After three days of silence in the house, not even ten minutes went by before one of our mother's longest best friends, Gloria, pulled up our driveway and let herself in. My brother was speaking on the phone to the others as she told me something had beckoned her spirit to get going that morning.

Learning that Gloria had hurried, driving two and a half hours with feelings of surety, and knowing I had also begun to strengthen my own connection to the underworld, I felt Beauty had already begun to conspire beyond life. Here she was composing and sending comfort to be received in harmony with her transition.

While others began to join us too, I noticed my mother's cat, named after the goddess Juno, began to hyperventilate in the crowded room. Her little mouth hung open, whiskers lifted off her teeth, tongue out, with fast breathing until she started to drool, like a panting dog gaping up at the bed.

Never before had I seen the kitty walk into a room full of strangers, or pant like it was 120 degrees. Nobody else noticed at first. I couldn't seem to do anything in my state of shock, however. Finally, watching, Gloria saw Juno struggling oddly, so she picked her up, petting her for a while as I remained transfixed, indeed, realizing I would be her new owner.

XXXII: ALLIGNMENT

I felt my emotional being under a weight burying me so I could not function. The ground of my existence seemed shattered to a level I had not known possible; beyond all comprehension. I was so upset at my precious mom's passing that I dangerously wanted to go with her. That is when she sent the first visual message to ease my pain. It was a picture of our family rocking chair. Her essence was in the image.

Suddenly I felt driven again for something. Small change would bring a subtle rise to my collapsed state. It was perfect, that rocking chair was where she would rock all her babies when needing to be soothed. I stood up without hesitation, picking myself up to leave the house on my own because I knew what the translation meant. Mumsy had shown me where to go.

I hadn't thought of it in more than a decade. That family heirloom had been stored within our old, one-room schoolhouse for years. The building was on the other side of the brook which ran constantly with spring water, flowing through the center of our parcel from the top to the bottom of the land. I walked barefoot across the side yard, then waded through the cold rumbling boundary.

The old bridge I would have used had been knocked down by a tremendous 100-year storm that came not long before. I navigated the rocks in the stream without care. Needing to be comforted in the way that only my own mother would understand, I took no notice of the freezing temperature, or where to step while I made my way across, then climbed using my hands also, up the grassy slope on the opposite side.

As I got closer to the sweet little brick building, I remembered how ancient it actually was. As far back as 1790, the school children must have had their lessons within its endearing, vintage, peach walls. Surely none of them would ever have imagined that I would come centuries later, searching for comfort. I did also think, however, that some of the children might have cried, and guessed the school teacher may have soothed them too.

There was something charming about the way the room had been built. The craftsmanship of the square one-story building could never go unnoticed. The single room had grandeur. Even though small, its sixteen-inch-wide wooden floor planks showed what great environmental resources our predecessors had at their disposal. Dark exposed beams attached by wedges and wooden pegs decorated the structure. Still standing with the original paint, the fading color was worn with time.

The entrance was weathered too. I climbed the granite steps to go inside. Built into the bricks were wooden repeating doors that had latch and hook handles. I closed the classroom door behind me while I left the outer open to swing.

Inside, the neglected rocking chair was still solid. It stood frozen in time, facing the one fireplace with a grand chimney hearth, built to warm the room which now had carried no warmth for over a century.

I made wet footprints as I approached it, dragging my feet through the dust built up on the floor. Pulling myself onto the old cushion, I curled up into the big carved wooden arms of the comforting rocking chair.

Its wood was chipped and softened by time and handling. The cushion was ripped and uneven. I didn't know if it was from rocking so many tearful children, or from mice chewing at it, but it didn't matter. Its wear, holes and cracks from abandonment didn't change the power it held for me. I was showing my Mom I was paying attention to her.

For an unknown amount of time, I rocked myself in the tattered old chair. As it coddled me, drifting in and out of full consciousness, further detail of the memories from Sundara and our previous lives together flooded into my mind for the first time.

I saw us at the sea cliff.

Flashes of light flickered between time periods. She laughed at me, looking down from her fancy stagecoach.

The responsibility of our life in Egypt came back to my memories as if it was not long ago.

I relearned about our fate as women of the woods.

Realizing our spiritual union more fully, I saw how she had sacrificed many times for me. That particular thought brought a cascade of recognized similarities. I pleaded aloud, *"Not again..."*

Seeing her taken from me before she was old enough to fully realize her legacy, I only knew we had been blessed to live peacefully for so long. A jolt came as I understood all her strength and mine combined toward our ultimate purpose. I kept my eyes tightly shut, not wanting to lose the thread.

I finally understood why she had been too afraid to come out as a spiritual person in this lifetime. Her suffering had been so recent. This time, she had lived more freely while I matured. Indeed, it was our special bond which ultimately gave power for both of us to liberate together beyond all fears, finally.

Aware now I was feeling through the vibrations of truth, it became clear to me that the soul I knew as my mother was Beauty. With a strong, regal essence, she guides with great love, forging with wisdom, while I humbly assist. In each lifetime she reawakens to further her gifts to the world, accepting all challenges to complete the overall dreamquest.

These memories occurred as senses and visions. I was giving myself completely to dreamwalking, learning how to connect with the underworld. The messages were flowing in so rapidly, I allowed no distractions while understanding my mother was teaching me how to reach her—better than dialing any phone. My intuition told me I would not be away from her ever again. Things were different now, yet it felt too incredible to believe through the weight of my intense grief.

Abruptly, I heard cars sweeping into the driveway. Even having others around, sending vibrations of intent to see me, was too much to ask. When more groups of people began to show up to help my family, I stayed away, wanting to be alone. No one could understand. I knew I had to be where I could keep my mind quieted, to stay close with her, just a while longer.

Unbearably, my eyes opened without feeling—it came time to leave the rocking chair. I dragged myself away from the solitude to return to the visitors who had come to pay their respects.

Walking carefully across the cold wet stones in the brook, I could feel all shapes and sizes with my bare toes. All of my lives were now reconnected in sensory memories. Somehow it came to me that, fully exposed, to feel everything in life was exactly how I had found Sundara in the first place.

Every sense was finally welcome, including the cumbersome ones. Comforted in knowing this was only one of many lives, my heart filled with something steady again. Most important was to continue to be united.

Vermont humidity and tears wet my face as I crossed the lawn again to re-enter the house. I made my way through the threshold saying, *"Thank you..."* distinctly feeling as though the delicate flower which held the door open until I returned was actually my mom's spirit, her energy holding it open just for me.

XXXIII: EMERLYE

Regarding life as a design, to become an artist of the universe, a person only has to color it.

Just two days before my mother's crossing, in response to our family's inquiries, and for the first time ever in history, the one gallery in Pomfret—the 'Artistree'—announced a last-minute opening in their coveted schedule. Such timing could not have been more perfect!

The coordinator offered to host the Emerlye Arts collection. My Aunt Edith and many who wanted to help were able to organize the showing, presenting the artist's legacy the very weekend after her passing.

The successful show opened with a prayer. Those who attended were so happy to have come. Everyone was aware, their beloved Cynthia's message to all: death is a rebirth.

A wise matriarch, she had also provided written instructions for exactly what she wanted everyone to sing at her ceremony downtown. Every soul who attended rang with the words, "Let it be," by the Beatles.

In the following difficult days, I worked on several of the coloring images. I wanted my mom's drawings all around me. My sister and I had split her vast collections of art supplies between us, so now, in front of our living room fireplace—revisiting where I had made art many times previously—I dumped all of what I had on the rug before me.

While I dazed, meditatively shading inside the black-and-white lines with color, I thought of how I would legally change my signature to reflect the way my heart felt. I held the mission of bringing Emerlye Arts to the world. Though it was too bad I couldn't have done it sooner, I was sure I should become the next Ms. Emerlye.

It wasn't about replacing her, or even trying to match her brilliance—how could anyone? It was about honoring her as her most devoted fan, the one who had been watching her in awe my entire life. She had a way of sweetly deflecting any admiration, treating even her biggest fans with the same modest shrug and warm smile. But in my heart, I knew I could take the torch she had lit, carry it forward, and keep her vision alive for as long as my hands could hold it.

Remembering the reason for my mother's decision to make her name change, I recalled how she had held focus for over a year on the subject as one of her longer dreamwalk intentions. She had commenced upon a spiritual embarkment, gathering omens and signs to collect her answer.

She wanted to find the future physical symbol of herself, as it would be written into life. For it to be something new, yet also holding the past. The letters that spelled out what she decided on were found one day while I was present, watching her sit at my grandmother's kitchen table. I saw her look through a large Webster's dictionary, choosing words that pleased her. She circled in pencil "to emerge," "to egress," adding letters also from my father's name, her children's surname, Lynch.

Several months later, still quietly grieving, I returned to Santa Cruz where my significant other, Tushar, had purchased a home. The incredible location perched to overlook a famous surf break on the Pacific Ocean.

I had fallen into deep depression and remained that way for some time. However wonderful our life was, Tushar noticed after weeks that I was not looking out the fancy windows.

For the first time in my life, I could not see beauty. I was critically overwhelmed, hiding from anything that made me feel any kind of emotion. Even good feelings were somehow still exhausting. I couldn't bear the feeling of anyone wanting from me, even a smile becoming too arduous.

On one particularly agonizing day, amid phone calls and persuasions through the door for me to come out for one event or another, my loving partner found me lying on the cold floor. I was looking up at the underside of my bed; crawling under it had felt like an appropriate place for my pain. He came underneath by me, asking me to join the world again, but I could not.

After several months of distraction, finally, I was left to myself. The aloneness helped me reach the answers I needed. I could focus on the waves as they hit the sea cliff repeatedly. Then, a youthful female voice spoke to me. I heard it utter the word, "Mom." Funny enough, the tone had an eye roll in it. I realized I, too, may one day have a daughter. Here she was, judging me for being ridiculous enough to need her already! I was selfishly relieved to see, like all who have come before me, one day any children of mine may have to sustain my return to ether, as is the way.

My loss was not so incomparable. From that moment on, I regained my determination, not to be depressed any longer, but to move forward with my journey. I finally allowed Tushar to take my hand, helping me leave the confines of the princess sweet I'd held myself within for weeks.

Following life's beauties, the way that had been taught to me, was my best way out from under the bed. Once Tushar pulled me up, we had not slowed ourselves with putting on our shoes when he walked me out the door. The connection with the earth and all my senses brought me through his front yard and beyond. Faithful and patient, he knew what I needed based upon what he remembered of the real me.

We went across the street to Pleasure Point Market for some goodies he knew would lighten my mood. Over where we sat by the cliffside afterward, I searched with hope to spot a glimpse of our favorite friendly otter who lived wild nearby.

We enjoyed our choice of ice cream cones together. Risen into the beautiful daylight shining down warmly, I felt Beauty guiding me to see nothing of the happy earth was going to fade just because I was dwelling in darkness.

Indeed, in order to remain my mother's darling girl who survived her, to be worthy of her legacy, brightness had to come from within. Resolved, I saw further truth. The turns of my labyrinth, my dreamwalk, would show more around the bend, if I could just keep one bare foot in front of the next; balancing across all things.

EPILOG

Metamorphosis has begun. I am now seen and known by my new, transformed name. The journey of my life has carried me from who I once was, through the vessel of art, into the new existence I now share with the world.

The unfolding of it all has felt like a slow-building symphony, the way serendipity often works, how kismet feels like unexpected perfection aligning at just the right time. That's the truth of life: things do eventually come together, like scattered puzzle pieces that, only in hindsight, reveal a great masterpiece we never knew we were helping to complete.

That's how I see my union with my mother and her brand—a divine, meant-to-be alignment. It captivates me deeply. Like two colors drawn into a cosmic clock, we were colored into time.

The synchronicities that followed her passing were magical, like hidden messages left on our path. One such moment arrived through a song, *Meant to Be* by Bebe Rexha, released around the same time as her transition. Its lyrics felt like a modern echo of a tune from The Beatles, as if the universe itself had composed the soundtrack to help me understand the beauty hidden within grief.

These strange and beautiful manifestations continued through Benevolence Bound, the only brand my mother and I created together. Even with its early success, I remember feeling as though the dragonflies—the quiet messengers of transformation—were asking me to dissolve before I could rise again.

And rise I did.

Not just as a daughter, but as the steward of her life's work—the next Ms. Emerlye.

It is not a title I take lightly. It is a living promise. I will carry her spirit into the future, keeping her art and her ethos alive in every hand that colors her lines, every heart that finds solace in her beauty.

Aligned with that vision, I often return to the medical caduceus my mother designed for our label. She drew a new version of the ancient symbol, one where, instead of twin serpents, a phoenix rises at the center. Unknowing of the future, her heart had chosen the perfect image of rebirth—a firebird ascending from its own ashes. In its tail feathers rests the universal saber of healing.

Considering everything, no example of cosmic alignment shines quite as brightly as what happened the year Beauty crossed into space. From her home in Vermont, a celestial gift awaited her—a message sent long before her life began.

On the year of her transcendence, 2017, on the very day of her birth, August 21, the sky itself delivered a masterpiece: the Great American Eclipse, a magnificent line of eternity drawn across the heavens by a streaking ancient star.

But stories do not truly end where the pages close.

Soon after the events you have just read, life delivered another moment that reshaped my path. My dear friend and former partner, Tushar, had his life taken from him unexpectedly. His death was another reminder of how fragile the human story can be, how suddenly the people we love can vanish from the chapters of our lives.

For nearly a decade I had built a career cultivating crops—learning the science, the discipline, and the relentless patience of agriculture. By many measures, that life was working.

But after that loss, something inside me changed with absolute clarity.

Regardless of whether that path was successful… regardless of whether it was logical or financially wise… I knew I could no longer give my life to anything else.

This was the work.

To step fully into the role that destiny had quietly prepared for me.

To become the next Ms. Emerlye.

To carry my mother's art forward so that its beauty might continue reaching people who, like me, have known the deep valleys of grief.

Because beauty has a mysterious power: it keeps the human spirit alive.

Today I am rebuilding and expanding the Emerlye Arts brand so that this body of work—her drawings, writings, philosophies, and healing imagery—can travel further than either of us could have taken it alone.

Every time someone purchases a coloring page, a book, or a piece of art from Emerlye Arts, they are not simply buying a product. They are helping this mission continue. They are helping beauty travel a little farther into the world.

If this story moved you, I welcome you to reach out.

Readers, collaborators, dreamers, and potential partners are all invited to write to me directly at: rachael@emerlyearts.com because stories like this are never built by one person alone.They are built by everyone who believes beauty still has a role to play in healing the world.

And if there is one thing I have learned through this journey, it is that beauty—once shared—has a way of multiplying far beyond the life of the person who first created it.

***

> *As the wind blows, with a greater sense of the world than what our minds understand, the release of spiritual energy reaches everywhere.*

- The Beginning

www.ingramcontent.com/pod-product-compliance
Lightning Source LLC
Chambersburg PA
CBHW030914080526
44589CB00010B/299